Shaken Stirred

BUT NOT

DETERRED

Vol. 3

Celebrating the Power of Human Spirit

GLOBAL INFLUENCERS

GLOBAL INFLUENCERS

GLOBAL INFLUENCERS PUBLISHING HOUSE
152 Prince Charles Cr, #17-12 Singapore 159013
Website: www.globalinfluencers.sg
Email: shikha@globalinfluencers.sg
First Published in Singapore by Global Influencers Publishing House 2025

Title: Shaken, Stirred But Not Deterred – Vol. 3
Celebrating The Power Of Human Spirit

ISBN: 978-981-17458-5-0 (Paperback)
978-981-17458-7-4 (Kindle)
978-981-17458-6-7 (Hardcover)

GLOBAL INFLUENCERS PUBLISHING HOUSE

CONTENTS

PREFACE

In a world filled with challenges, uncertainties, and transformative experiences, we often discover that our personal journeys are intertwined with the stories of others. *"Shaken, Stirred but Not Deterred, Celebrating The Power Of Human Spirit - Vol. 3"* celebrates the resilience of individuals from diverse backgrounds, showcasing their inspiring narratives that illuminate their paths to overcoming adversity. This anthology serves as a powerful reminder that every story is essential and that the lessons learned can create ripples of change in our communities.

As you delve into each chapter, we urge you not only to read but also to reflect and engage actively. Each contributor invites you to become advocates for positive change—whether by raising awareness about issues affecting marginalised groups, particularly girls and women, or by supporting organisations that champion their rights and education. The beauty of these personal stories lies in their ability to spark meaningful conversations, urging us to think critically about our roles in creating a fairer world.

We must recognise that everyone possesses the power to challenge injustices and amplify the voices often silenced. Together, we can foster a culture of respect, equality, and empowerment, not only for ourselves but for future generations. This book emphasises that the path to self-discovery is marked by resilience and an unwavering commitment to our dreams, regardless of the obstacles we face.

Moreover, the contributions within this anthology reflect shared themes of personal growth, financial wellness, and the importance of maintaining balanced well-being across various dimensions of life. They remind us that true success is not defined solely by professional accomplishments but by the richness of our experiences, relationships, and inner peace.

As we share the journeys of 18 authors within this anthology, we hope to illustrate that moments of struggle and doubt can serve as catalysts for transformation. The commitment to empowering others fuels the drive to create a positive impact within the community and encourages readers to take those same steps toward realising their potential.

We invite you to embark on this journey of inspiration and self-reflection, reminding you that within each of us lies the capacity to effect change. Together, let us embrace the challenges, celebrate the victories, and rise above the struggles, knowing that we are never alone in our pursuits.

SINGAPORE CHILDREN'S SOCIETY

Children's
SOCIETY
Caring for the Future

Founded in 1952, the mission of Singapore Children's Society is to bring relief and happiness to children in need. The Society protects and nurtures children and youth of all races and religions.

Singapore Children's Society currently operates 10 service centres, offering services in the four categories of: Vulnerable Children and Youth, Children and Youth Services, Family Services, and Research and Advocacy.

Funds raised through the sale of this volume will support the work of the Society which includes being a voice for our children and their future.

We are grateful for the trust that the authors and publishers of this book have shown in supporting our work. Without their collective voices this book would not exist.

For further information and to support the Society, visit our website at https://www.childrensociety.org.sg/

Story One

AGAINST ALL ODDS

The Struggles and Triumphs of Girl Child Rescue.

In the heart of Narok County, Narok South Sub-County, I witness a quiet battle unfold every school holiday, especially during the long December break. This battle involves the unwavering determination of many stakeholders in the child protection space, including myself, as we confront the deep-rooted traditions that hold the lives of countless young Maasai girls hostage to harmful cultural practices such as child marriage, child booking/beading, Female Genital Mutilation (FGM), and child labour. My journey with the Light of Life Organisation offers a glimmer of hope for these girls trapped in a cycle of abuse and neglect. I am committed to creating positive change and believe wholeheartedly that education is fundamental to a child's future.

In this chapter, I want to share the challenges that I, along with many other rescuers, face in our efforts to protect these vulnerable girls. I will discuss the barriers we encounter and highlight the inspiring success stories that emerge when a girl is given the opportunity to access education. Breaking free from traditional cultural norms empowers these girls to make independent, informed decisions about their lives. I know that the road to freedom is not easy, but the impact of completing this journey is life-changing.

THE STRUGGLES AND STIGMA: A MAASAI GIRL'S LIFE

To fully appreciate the significance of the work being undertaken, it is crucial to understand the cultural and societal challenges facing young Maasai girls in Narok County and other regions. For many years, families in our pastoralist communities have viewed the education of girls as secondary to that of boys. We often see girls regarded as commodities to be married off early, a practice reinforced by tradition and poverty. In our communities, girls are expected to bear children and contribute to the household from a young age.

In addition to child marriage, Female Genital Mutilation (FGM) remains a deeply ingrained practice in many Maasai communities here in Narok. This ritual, often performed on girls as young as 10 or 11 years old, marks the transition from childhood to adulthood. However, it carries significant health risks and emotional trauma with lifelong consequences.

Child labour, particularly in the form of early domestic work or as herders, as well as sand harvesting, deprives girls of the chance to receive an education and experience a proper childhood. This combination of child marriage, FGM, and child labour creates a toxic environment where these girls' potential is stifled before it can even begin to bloom.

THE PATHFINDER: LIGHT OF LIFE ORGANIZATION

Amidst the harsh realities faced by young Maasai girls, I have dedicated my life to changing their futures. I work with the Light of Life Organization, a non-governmental organisation focused on rescuing girls from the horrors of child marriage, Female Genital Mutilation (FGM), and child labour, while also providing them with the education they desperately need to break free from the cycle of poverty and exploitation.

However, my journey has not been without its struggles. From the very beginning, my work has been met with resistance. The cultural beliefs that underpin these practices are deeply entrenched in our community, and many families are unwilling to allow their daughters to be rescued. I often face threats from parents who are desperate to marry off their daughters or to see them undergo the painful ritual of FGM. The stigma surrounding a girl who escapes these practices is equally dangerous, as the community sometimes labels them as outcasts or disrespectful.

Despite these challenges, I remain steadfast in my commitment to saving as many girls as possible. I work tirelessly to negotiate with families, educate the community about the dangers of FGM and child marriage, and offer an alternative path for these girls through education.

THE DANGEROUS JOURNEY OF RESCUING GIRLS

The process of rescuing a girl from the grips of child marriage, FGM, or child labour is far from simple. It's not just about offering a safe space; the logistics involved are complex, and I often face physical and emotional dangers myself.

The initial challenge is securing the girls' departure from their homes. While many seek to escape these harmful practices, they are deeply fearful of the consequences if caught. Many of these girls have been socialised to believe that their future is defined by marriage and motherhood, rather than education or self-empowerment. In some cases, they have been so traumatised by their circumstances that they are afraid to leave, fearing punishment or rejection from their families.

Once the girls become aware that their parents are discussing the possibility of mutilation, they begin to remain vigilant, watching for warning signs before attempting to escape. Some overhear their fathers speaking to their mothers about the practice, while others notice suitors arriving with ornaments or beads to secure their commitment. In some instances, their mothers privately alert them to be cautious, signalling that their fathers are preparing them for marriage.

As the threat of these practices becomes imminent, the girls start considering potential escape routes. Some flee at night while their family members are still asleep, others run away from school and do not return home for the holidays, while some escape early in the morning, seeking refuge in the bushes, with their class teachers, a pastor, or even at a local police station.

In some very unfortunate and tragic cases, girls find themselves subjected to mutilation, becoming victims of their circumstances. Even after undergoing the cut, some do not lose hope; they manage to escape once they are healed, unwilling to accept a life of marriage that is thrust upon them.

Once a girl escapes from these harmful practices, I and other rescuers face the significant challenge of transporting her to a safe location. In rural areas like Narok, this often involves traversing long distances across difficult terrain, with limited access to proper roads and unreliable communication networks. Additionally, it requires continuous vigilance, as we risk being intercepted by family members or community members who may attempt to prevent the girl's escape.

One of the most challenging aspects of this work is the emotional toll it takes on me and the rest of the rescue team. Many girls rescued from child marriage or FGM carry deep physical and psychological scars. I have witnessed firsthand the trauma these girls endure and the resilience they demonstrate once given the chance to heal and pursue their dreams. It is not uncommon for me to comfort a girl experiencing profound guilt or shame for having left her family, or to deal with the anger of a girl who feels betrayed by her community.

The process of healing is long and difficult, but the rewards are immense. After being rescued, the girls are enrolled in schools and provided with everything they need to succeed—tuition fees, uniforms, books, and most importantly, emotional and psychological support. With this foundation, the girls begin their journey toward a brighter future.

REINTEGRATION

The joy that fills the air when the girls are finally reunited with their families after a period of silence and recovery is indescribable. Many parents feel guilty for the wrongs they have committed, and they always wish to right all the wrongs they have done to their children. They promise not to violate their daughters further, allowing them to pursue their dreams and achieve their goals. It brings me immense happiness to see these young girls thriving, living their lives to the fullest, and following their dreams.

THE TRANSFORMATIVE POWER OF EDUCATION: A NEW LEASE ON LIFE

One of the most powerful success stories to emerge from the work of the Light of Life Organization is the profound impact education has had on the girls we rescue. When given the opportunity to attend school, many of them flourish, proving to themselves and their communities that they are capable of achieving greatness.

Take, for example, the story of Amina*. I rescued her at the age of 13 from an arranged marriage. Her family had already begun preparing for her to undergo FGM and marry a much older man. Amina was terrified of the life that lay ahead of her. However, after I intervened, she was able to escape her fate. With the support of Light of Life, Amina was enrolled in secondary school and later pursued a degree in nursing. Today, she stands as an inspiration to other girls in her community and is a powerful advocate against FGM and child marriage.

Another remarkable success story is that of Faith*, a girl who had been forced into child labour as a herder. She had no opportunity to attend school, and the demands of her work crushed her dreams for the future. After I and my team rescued her, Faith thrived in school and eventually earned a scholarship to attend a university in Nairobi. Today, she works as a teacher and mentors' other young girls who face similar struggles.

Then there is Angel*, who was at risk of dropping out of school due to financial constraints, while her father intended to marry her off at the age of 14. Angel had a strong passion for education. After my intervention, she was able to continue her studies. In 2017, Angel excelled academically, topping her class, and went on to attend a public university, where she graduated with first-class honours in Bachelor of Commerce. She was awarded a scholarship to pursue her Master's degree in the UK and is now giving back to the community by sponsoring a girl's education.

These success stories are a testament to the incredible transformation that can occur when a girl is given the tools she needs to succeed. It is not just about education; it is about restoring dignity, self-worth, and hope to girls who have been robbed of their futures.

**Not their real names*

THE ROAD AHEAD

While my work and that of the Light of Life Organization have made a tremendous impact in Kajiado and Narok Counties, there is still much work to be done. The challenges we face are immense, and the journey to ending harmful practices such as child marriage, FGM, and child labour is long. However, each life saved, and each girl empowered is a victory worth celebrating.

The fight for the girl child in Kajiado and Narok Counties requires not only the dedication of rescuers like me but also the collective effort of the community, the government, and organisations worldwide. It is only through sustained education, advocacy, and support that we can achieve real, lasting change.

For every girl who is rescued from the bonds of tradition, there is a world of possibility waiting for her. With the power of education and the support of compassionate individuals, the girls of Narok County can break free from the chains that hold them back and rise to become the women they were always meant to be.

In the end, it is not just the girls who are saved—it is the entire community. By empowering girls to take control of their futures, we pave the way for a brighter, more prosperous future for all.

A CALL TO ACTION

I urge everyone reading this to become advocates for change in their communities. Raise awareness about the harmful practices affecting girls, engage in meaningful conversations, and educate others on the importance of girls' rights and education. Support local organisations that work towards these goals, whether through donations, volunteering, or sharing their messages on social media. Your voice matters: even small actions can lead to significant change. Together, we can create an environment where every girl is empowered to dream, achieve, and break free from the constraints of tradition.

Each of us has the power to challenge these injustices and amplify the voices of those who are often silenced. By fostering a culture of respect and equality, we can inspire future generations to continue the fight. Join us in this vital effort to transform lives and build a better future for all.

ABOUT THE AUTHOR

Evelyne Nakola was born and raised in Narok South, Kenya, where pastoralism is the main economic activity. As the eldest of eight siblings, she faced significant challenges, especially after narrowly escaping the harmful practice of Female Genital Mutilation (FGM) at age 12. Witnessing the traumatic effects of FGM and early marriages on her cousins deepened her resolve. Despite societal pressures, her father refused to allow his daughters to undergo FGM, leading to rejection and hostility from their community.

Recognised for her passion for education, Evelyne received sponsorship for her undergraduate studies from the late Kenyan President, Daniel Toroitich Arap Moi. This opportunity inspired her to support young girls affected by FGM and child marriages, leading her to establish the Light of Life Organization. Through her work, she has supported over 700 girls, emphasising education and advocacy for women's rights. Evelyne's unwavering commitment to transform lives earned her the prestigious Global Women of Influence Awards in 2024.

YOU CAN CONNECT WITH EVELYNE AT:

Website: *https://lightoflife.or.ke/*
Facebook: *https://www.facebook.com/p/Light-of-life-organization-100070681382400/*
Email: *evenakola14@gmail.com*

Story Two

A RISING PHOENIX

How Mindset and Faith Propel Success.

I grew up as the second daughter among five children to my military father and my mother, who was a teacher. Due to my father's military job, we moved frequently, which meant I studied in different states during my lower and upper primary years as well as my secondary school years. In my pre-teen years, my father was transferred again, but when he reported for duty at his new post, he suffered a stroke that affected his speech. He was flown abroad for treatment, but after a couple of months, his speech was not restored. Consequently, he retired and was relieved of his duties.

This marked the beginning of my mother's journey as the main caretaker at home. I watched the dynamics of the household change, which had a significant impact on me. As a young girl, I saw her life transform, with most of the dependency now on her. Although my father was a pensioner, my industrious mother had to combine her teaching job with several businesses, including a hair salon, bakery, and drinks shop, to provide our family with a decent living.

During weekends and holidays, my siblings and I assisted her in her businesses, which allowed me to learn hairdressing and nail painting skills at the young age of 13. I also helped in the drinks shop and in baking cakes and pastries; we were very hands-on kids. It was hard watching my mother work tirelessly to ensure the family had a decent living. My dad was now living with the effects of his stroke, and his pension salary, combined with my mother's income from her salary and multiple businesses, helped raise all of us to become university graduates now living with our own families. All of these experiences shaped me into the woman I am today—a serial entrepreneur who works hard and is not overly dependent on anyone, just in case life throws me a curveball.

Because my mother had to take care of my sick dad and my younger siblings, I had to grow up quickly in some ways. For instance, after finishing secondary school, I waited for two years because I needed to re-sit my university entry examination due to an initial score that didn't meet the requirements for my undergraduate course. When I retook the exam and achieved a higher score, I had to travel alone at the age of 17 to the far north—a twelve-hour bus ride to my chosen university, Ahmadu Bello University, Zaria—to secure my admission.

It was a scary move for me because I had never traveled on my own before. When I arrived at my destination, it was late at night, and my father's colleague, with whom I thought I would be staying, wasn't in town. However, I have always had a close relationship with God, and He guides me constantly. When I asked questions, I found another of my dad's colleagues on the same street, and that was how I secured a place to stay for the few days I had on that trip.

The courage it took to embark on that journey alone gave me the confidence to know that I could accomplish anything I set my heart on—even at such a young age. A similar experience occurred a few years later when I had to travel across the nation for my National Youth Service, which is a compulsory service to the nation after graduating from university. It takes courage and fearlessness to leave your comfort zone, embark on a journey to a new land and among new people, and try to live there at such a young age.

During my time at university, I focused on hard work and determination, determined not to let my family down. I studied diligently to complete my courses in one sitting and aimed for a higher grade. Motivated by a classmate's encouragement, I believed I could achieve a second-class upper degree. With the support of my boyfriend and classmates, I dedicated myself to my studies and successfully graduated as the only female among the top five students in the Economics department that year.

After completing my National Youth Service, I got married to my boyfriend from the university and became pregnant immediately afterward. Being an energetic person, I decided that I needed to get a job—I didn't want to be a stay-at-home mom. I applied to one of the biggest telecom companies in Nigeria. However, by the third stage of my interview, they discovered that I was pregnant and discontinued my application process. This was quite heartbreaking for me, but it didn't deter me.

I applied to the civil service, and just three weeks after having my first baby, I left my child under my mother's care and travelled to my state of origin for the interview. Despite all the inconvenience and passing with a very high score, I still didn't get the job because applicants with connections to high government officials were favoured.

Disappointed but undeterred, I ventured into business. In my first foray into business in 2004, my now ex-husband and I started a fast-food business called Laritas Food and Confectionery. We set it up in a remote area, but after a year of running the business, we faced numerous challenges due to its poor location and our business inexperience, leading to its failure. I then travelled to Dubai, purchased gold jewellery and women's clothing, and brought them back to sell in Abuja.

I sold out the women's wear, but the jewellery was difficult to sell. So, I decided to invest in the Mary Kay cosmetics business, which was introduced to me by my sister, and I excelled in the business for a couple of years, selling products door-to-door and gaining a substantial number of clients in the corporate world. Even while pregnant with my children, I wore my stiletto heels and sold my cosmetics.

This success in the Mary Kay business propelled me to upgrade from door-to-door sales and set up a brick-and-mortar business. In 2009, I took beauty training at The Beauty Academy in London, and in Abuja, Nigeria, I established my salon and spa business, The Laritas Beauty Spa. I ran this business for eight years before closing due to the major challenge of constantly searching for new clients; when stylists resigned, they often took my clients with them, leading to a constant struggle.

A year after I opened the salon/spa, in 2010, I took on a franchise in the restaurant business. After three years of running the Chinese restaurant franchise, I ended the franchise, changed the name, and continued to operate solely as Marcoriano Chinese Restaurant. Although it has been quite challenging to own and run a Chinese restaurant in Abuja, primarily due to the heavy dependence on foreign products and my decision to quit using a Chinese chef earlier in the business due to significantly high non-citizen taxes, it has been a rewarding experience running the business for the past 14 years to date.

The business has thrived through three different government regimes and has endured really tough seasons. I couldn't pay my rent at my main branch during one of the government changes, and my landlord shut off my water and electricity, abruptly closing my business. I depended on my subsidiary branch for a few years, struggling to keep the business running without external funds to cover expenses and salaries.

The nation's economy was experiencing a downturn, and many businesses struggled to keep their doors open, but nevertheless, I persisted, and Marcoriano Chinese Restaurant remains open to this day—shaken, stirred, but definitely not deterred.

Being the serial entrepreneur that I am and a lover of fashion, I started my own fashion brand, Zarita Kouture, in 2012. The business has gone through different phases, initially producing and selling ready-to-wear items, then adding bespoke custom clothing and a fashion training academy over the years. It has evolved from a brick-and-mortar store to an online store and now operates strictly by appointment. The business faced challenging times, particularly during the COVID period, but it has continued to persevere and remain in existence.

During the COVID-19 year, the world shut down for three months, and so did my businesses. It was a trying period for me and all business owners worldwide, as the bulk of my daily expenses came from the income I earned from my businesses. My first challenge was with my staff; they weren't allowed to work during the lockdown period, and I felt obliged to ensure they earned at least half of their salaries each month so they could get by as they faced the challenges of the lockdown. These were expenses paid without any earnings, leading to a heavy reliance on my savings.

In my fashion business, an income opportunity arose, and I quickly seized it: the market for sewing face masks. Since the cost of buying a ready-made face mask was higher than that of locally sewn, washable and reusable masks, this opportunity was timely. We received orders to produce masks for private individuals and also in bulk for events and gatherings throughout the COVID period. The pandemic also prompted many business owners, myself included, to think creatively, leading to new ways of conducting business—especially with the introduction of online services and transactions.

During this period, my fashion business transitioned away from brick-and-mortar services to focus on online sales. I increased social media marketing and shifted to appointment-only physical services, which allowed me to save on rent. In the food business, we experienced increased online orders as people became more comfortable with takeout, so I reduced my service staff and ensured that my website was fully equipped as an e-commerce site to facilitate smooth transactions.

As a philanthropist, I established the StellaRita Awelle Humanitarian Foundation in 2021, using it officially to carry out most of my yearly charity work and to engage in corporate social responsibility initiatives within my community, focusing particularly on the welfare and empowerment of women and youths. In 2024, the foundation hosted the Zarita Fashion and Arts Fusion, a platform that showcased and empowered talented but previously unknown African fashion and arts creatives. This event provided an excellent opportunity to highlight these creatives and give them the financial and media support they needed to launch their own small businesses. It also exposed the foundation to potential sponsorships from major organisations, and I am hopeful that this is just the beginning of greater things to come for these creatives. My vision and mindset are now going global. I am receiving international recognition, and nations are calling on me as I move steadily forward.

Despite the numerous hours I dedicate to running my businesses, I always prioritise my greatest love and passion—my children and family. My family is my foundation, the heart of my life, and their well-being comes first in all my daily decision-making and choices. Life has presented its challenges, both personal and business challenges but yet I, StellaRita Awelle Nwachukwu Asogwa, refuse to succumb to failure. Each setback becomes an opportunity; even when I stumble, I rise again, fuelled by my unwavering faith in God.

I want anyone reading this to know that your journey truly begins within your mind. The path to success is often influenced by your mindset. Whether you push forward or choose to quit hinges on how you perceive obstacles. In any business or career you pursue, challenges are inevitable. It's crucial to recognise that these difficulties are but seasonal experiences that will eventually pass. No challenge lasts forever.

While these trials may be tough, they carry valuable lessons that can shape your growth. Embrace each setback as a chance to learn and evolve. The experience gained from overcoming adversity equips you to move forward and reach your next level of success. Remember, persistence is key—do not give up too quickly. Instead, approach each hurdle with resilience and maintain the courage to keep pursuing your dreams, no matter the obstacles you face.

ABOUT THE AUTHOR

StellaRita Awelle Nwachukwu Asogwa is an accomplished Igbo entrepreneur and philanthropist from Nkwerre LGA in Imo State, Nigeria. With two decades of experience in the food and fashion industries, she has made a significant impact in these sectors both locally and internationally. A graduate of Ahmadu Bello University and holding an MBA from the Business School Netherlands, StellaRita is a Fellow of the International Institute of Strategy and Development (FIISD), the Chartered Institute of Arts Professionals (FCIAP), and Brand Management of Nigeria (FBMN).

Her designs in fashion have been showcased at runway events in Nigeria, the UK, Paris, and South Africa. Through her StellaRita Awelle Humanitarian Foundation, an accredited member of the World Peace Organisation, she supports schools and local communities by providing essential resources to women, widows, and youth. She also received the Global Women of Influence Award 2024 for her significant contribution to society.

YOU CAN CONNECT WITH STELLARITA AT:

LinkedIn: *https://www.linkedin.com/in/amb-dr-hc-stellarita-awelle-asogwa-fibm-fiisd-fciap-jp-b0147761/*
Website: *https://stellaritaawellefoundation.org/*
Email: *stelarit@yahoo.com*

Story Three

BEYOND THE NUMBERS

How Financial Literacy Transforms Lives.

As I adjusted my headset, I wasn't just preparing for my first podcast recording—I was stepping into a new chapter, one where my voice could bring about meaningful change. A mix of excitement and nervousness washed over me. This was my first podcast recording, and it was personal. It was the first time I had the chance to talk about finance in a way that truly mattered to me, connecting it to people's everyday lives. It was an opportunity to speak directly to individuals about a topic that had significantly shaped the course of my life: financial wellbeing.

I had spent years working in finance—analysing numbers, guiding companies, and helping individuals make informed decisions—but this felt different. I wasn't just talking about balance sheets and forecasts; I was sharing a vision for empowering others to take control of their financial future, especially women, who often face unique challenges in this space.

As I hit the record button and started speaking, I realised my journey had led me to this moment—not just as a finance professional, but as a voice for change. This podcast was about more than finance; it was about wellbeing, empowerment, and creating a future where people felt confident in their financial decisions. And it all started here, with one conversation I hoped would make a difference.

Growing up, I never imagined I would one day speak about finance with such conviction. My relationship with money was complex, shaped by both personal experiences and cultural expectations. Like many, I learned the hard way about managing finances and realised that financial literacy was not just about numbers—it was about life choices and opportunities.

I was born into a well-off family during the Lebanese civil war, one of the most difficult situations one could imagine. Nowhere was safe, and all we could focus on was survival. As I grew older, the country's situation worsened, and the wealthy family I once knew was no longer the same.

Moving to a different neighbourhood and changing schools, while living with the bare minimum as an 8-year-old, was not what I had expected. With less money and my parents working intense jobs, their focus shifted entirely to making ends meet. As a result, emotional and mental wellbeing took a backseat.

My mother is the most remarkable person I know—she did everything in her power to raise us well. My father, on the other hand, was more challenging. When I was nine, he insisted that I wear the hijab, despite my resistance. I was so young at the time, and this experience profoundly shaped who I am today.

As I began to envision my future, I dreamed of becoming a nutritionist. This likely stemmed from my struggles with being overweight and wanting to help others achieve a healthy body image, thereby avoiding the bullying I had faced. However, my parents' financial situation hadn't improved, and I had to make a difficult choice: either follow my dreams or study what we could afford and make a dream of it. Money dictated so many of my decisions—what university

I attended, my major, my social life, even my hobbies. It was all about money. And so, I chose finance. Money is powerful, and I wanted to take control of it.

After graduating with my Finance degree, I was driven to establish myself in the corporate world. I dedicated myself to continuous learning and skill development because I believed that the more proficient I became, the greater my financial success would be. With that financial success came power and confidence—both of which I craved after years of feeling restricted. Achieving financial independence meant no longer relying on anyone, and it gave me the freedom to make decisions that aligned with my true self. One of the first significant decisions I made was to take off the hijab. For me, it had never been about religious belief, but rather about the pressure to conform to an identity that wasn't mine. Removing it was a powerful step toward reclaiming my authenticity and shaping my own path.

I moved through several jobs, working hard and long hours, until I found an opportunity for international exposure. It wasn't long before I found myself on planes, traveling for projects, and finally relocating to Dubai after two years.

Living alone abroad as a young Arab woman was a challenge. Many people expected me to fail, and the journey wasn't easy. I lost jobs a few times, was far from the people I loved, and had to face these challenges on my own. Still, I kept going. Nothing could stop me, though I was so busy that I didn't have time to reflect on how I was making it through—until COVID hit.

The year 2020 was, without question, the most difficult year of my life. I lost my job, a career I had poured so much of myself into, and at the same time, I ended an eight-year toxic and abusive relationship. It was a devastating double blow that left me feeling like I had lost everything at once. There were moments when the weight of it all felt unbearable, like I was drowning in an overwhelming sea of uncertainty and pain. But somehow, deep inside, something kept me going—perhaps a small, flickering hope that I could find myself again.

Emotionally, I was shattered. Losing my job shook my confidence, and ending the relationship forced me to confront the years of emotional abuse I had buried. The person I had become felt like a stranger, someone who had lived under the weight of others' expectations and control for too long. The grief wasn't just about losing what I had—it was about realising how much of myself I had sacrificed. Every day felt like a battle, not just to survive, but to rediscover who I was beyond the roles I had played in my job and relationship.

As I navigated through the pain, there were small but significant moments that became turning points. I remember one evening, sitting alone and reflecting on everything that had happened. I could feel the exhaustion from years of trying to hold everything together. It was in that quiet moment of surrender that I realised I didn't have to hold it all anymore. Letting go didn't mean I was weak—it meant I was ready to rebuild.

I started by focusing on myself for the first time in years. Therapy helped me unpack the layers of self-doubt and fear that had accumulated over the years. I faced hard truths, acknowledging how I had allowed others to dictate my worth and my path. With each session, I felt a little lighter and a little stronger. I began setting boundaries, not just with others but with myself—no longer would I accept anything less than what I deserved.

2020 tested me in ways I never imagined, but it was also the year that taught me resilience. It showed me that even in the darkest moments, there is a spark within us that refuses to be extinguished. "That year didn't break me; it built me."

I soon landed my dream job in aviation and continued soaring ahead. Through therapy, I discovered my inner strength—that true resilience comes from within. I realised that I am invincible, able to rise from the ashes. I had always been there for myself and for others, and I understood that independence was key. The more independent I became, the stronger I felt. I learned to love my life and began seeing opportunities where I once saw challenges. I took up new hobbies I couldn't afford as a child and found peace of mind in the ocean by becoming a scuba diver.

It all came down to one undeniable truth: being financially well is essential. At that moment, I knew I wanted the world to understand how important it is to be independent and financially secure. I started seeing a reflection of my younger self in every woman I met. I listened to their stories and struggles, and they always led to the same question: Are you financially well?

Alongside my corporate job, my new goal in life became helping younger generations become self-reliant and independent. I aimed to be a positive role model and assist others in living their best lives. Individual well-being is crucial, yet attaining a well-lived life can be harder than it seems. When we think about health and well-being, we typically consider the physical, mental, and emotional aspects. But there's another critical aspect that has gained recognition over the last decade: financial wellness.

Avoiding financial overextension can also help prevent emotional burnout. While saying "no" to plans and obligations can be difficult, taking on too much can lead to burnout, which negatively affects overall health.

I started educating others about financial well-being through my blogs and talks, offering tips and guidance. I'm passionate about supporting younger people, especially women, in taking that first step towards financial independence and wellness.

As I reflect on my journey, one lesson stands out above all: financial well-being is deeply intertwined with our overall well-being. It's not just about having money; it's about the freedom and confidence that comes from knowing you are in control of your financial future. For me, every step—whether it was overcoming personal challenges, navigating the corporate world, or enduring the hardships of 2020—has underscored the power of financial independence.

Financial wellness is not a luxury but a necessity. It allows us to say "no" to situations that don't serve us, protect our emotional and mental health, and create space for opportunities that align with our goals and values. By managing our finances wisely, we reduce the risk of burnout and open the door to a life where we are not weighed down by stress but empowered to make meaningful choices.

Through my podcast, blogs, and speaking engagements, I've made it my mission to share this message, especially with young people and women who, like me, face unique financial challenges. I believe that financial literacy is the key to unlocking confidence and independence, and I hope to continue guiding others on this path.

My story is one of resilience, adaptation, and growth. I learned that it's not about avoiding the fall, but about how you rise each time. Financial wellness was my stepping stone to reclaiming my power, and I want it to be the foundation for others to do the same. As I continue to grow in my career and in life, my goal remains clear: to inspire others to take control of their financial futures, build resilience, and ultimately live the life they choose, not the one dictated by financial limitations.

As I wrapped up that first podcast episode, I realised that my story wasn't just about financial lessons—it was about resilience, growth, and the power of taking control. Now, I invite you to take action.

Start by assessing where you stand financially and identifying small, meaningful steps toward improvement. Invest in your financial education through books, podcasts, or workshops. Surround yourself with mentors and like-minded individuals who inspire and support your journey. Most importantly, don't be afraid to share your own story—

because when we speak up, we create ripples of change. Empower yourself to take charge of your financial future, and in doing so, inspire others to do the same.

Together, we can build a future where financial wellness is not a privilege, but a shared goal. And if my story helps even one person take that first step, then every challenge I've faced will have been worth it.

ABOUT THE AUTHOR

Noura Zein is a seasoned finance professional with nearly two decades of experience, marked by her resilience and commitment to fostering financial independence. Her expertise spans multiple industries and includes leading financial strategies, guiding risk management, and driving expansion efforts in international markets. Noura's personal journey has inspired her mission to champion financial well-being and empower women through financial literacy, building confidence and resilience.

While her path to success has included challenges, these experiences have intensified her dedication to mentoring others, particularly women facing unique financial and professional hurdles. Noura's core belief is that financial wellness goes beyond money; it represents freedom, peace of mind, and the ability to make empowered choices.

With a focus on advocating for financial independence, she inspires others to take control of their financial journeys and embrace their potential, encouraging a generation of women to thrive in every aspect of life.

YOU CAN CONNECT WITH NOURA AT:

LinkedIn: *https://www.linkedin.com/in/noura-zein-57510131/*
Email: *nourazein@hotmail.com*

Story Four

BEYOND THE VENEER OF SUCCESS

Living a Balanced Life with Self-Compassion.

Like many of my peers, I was raised to follow a common life path which I was taught is the blueprint for success: a good student, excellent grades, a prestigious degree, and a well-paying job. I diligently followed this script. As a management professional, I furthered my career by moving across the Middle East region, pursuing better opportunities & professional growth. I progressed very well in my career, managing highly profitable businesses within different firms, and possessing a distinguished record of achievements that defined my success. Work and career were my top priority, I was always chasing more growth and better opportunities to fulfil my increased demands. This was the expected narrative, the roadmap to a successful life – or so I thought!!

A MIRAGE OF SUCCESS

It was another 6 AM alarm, rushing me to work. My day was a routine cycle of a morning commute, stream of meetings, overflowing inbox and endless to-do list. I was trapped in a typical 9-to-5 working day, evenings were spent catching up on carryover work, and weekends were quickly passing for another busy Monday. My life was circling around work & career growth in a continuous chase of my endless ambitions. Over the years, a feeling of dissatisfaction & unhappiness was growing inside me, accompanied by anxiety and a constant sense of unease. My body started to rebel, protesting with exhaustion and a nagging sense of dread. I ignored the warning signs, pushing myself harder to do more, attempting to secure my next promotion & craving for additional income to fulfill my lifestyle growing needs.

One night, it all came crashing down, I experienced a severe medical condition that was a forced detour of my daily routine. I suffered from severe burnout, accompanied by high fever, difficulty in breathing, severe body pain, and persistent pressure in my chest, leaving me weak and disoriented. The vibrant hues of the world around me faded into a monotonous gray with a gradual loss of consciousness and suddenly, I found myself in complete darkness.

I opened my eyes to the sterile environment of the hospital, cut off from the constant demands of work, unstoppable notifications, and endless personal demands. A profound silence descended that was broken by the rhythmic beeping of the heart monitor. For the first time, I was confronted by the fragility of my health, fear, anxiety, and a deep sense of regret washed over me. Only then I realised the reality of what I have been chasing, it was nothing but a mirage of success.

THE BLOSSOMING OF A NEW LIFE

Disconnected from the outside world, faced by my own thoughts. I began to question everything, my values, my priorities, the very definition of success that was only defined by my work & professional growth.

Amidst this despair, a glimmer of hope emerged. My mother comforted me with her words, encouraging me to rebuild my strength & uprise. Her words struck a chord deep within me, an awaking moment made me realise what I had sacrificed in my relentless pursuit of success. I was living a very unbalanced life, my health was deteriorating, my mind was clouded with anxiety, my relationships became an afterthought, and my spiritual life was fading away. These were the seeds of awakening that led me to see my life through a different lens. This experience ignited the spark inside me to embark on a journey of self-discovery, prompting me to re-evaluate my life and rebuild it from the ground up.

Leaving the hospital, I felt a newfound sense of clarity fuelled with hope. This marked the beginning of my journey of self-discovery. Initially, I was unsure of where to begin. However, after thoughtful research, I realised the need for a holistic approach to examine my life. I started by identifying my priorities under seven key dimensions of my well-being that required better attention, then diagnosed each of them seeking concrete resolutions with a strong hope to live a new balanced life of well-being. The seven key dimensions of well-being are: Physical, Intellectual, Occupational, Family, Social, Financial & Spiritual.

THE ROADMAP TO RECOVERY

This holistic approach was the road map that put me back on track as soon as I began to diagnose each dimension and then act to fix it. This roadmap helped me to become conscious of how to live a balanced lifestyle while being a better version of myself.

Now, let us begin with the first dimension:

1-PHYSICAL WELL-BEING

As I have struggled through a hard medical condition, it was a tough lesson for me to start looking after my health. I started to prioritise my physical wellness, which was an afterthought for a long time amidst my focus on work and career; I began by nourishing my body with whole foods, replacing processed snacks & junk food with fruits, vegetables, and whole grains while following simple nutrition habits without exhausting myself with complex diet plans. Additionally, I started incorporating regular exercise into my routine by short walks while gradually increasing the intensity and duration. I also prioritised quality sleep, ensuring I got enough rest to recharge and rejuvenate. This renewed focus on my physical well-being had a profound impact on my overall health and energy levels, allowing me to approach life with renewed vigour and enthusiasm. The key action here is to start taking small and simple steps consistently without overwhelming myself with a perfect routine.

2-INTELLECTUAL WELL-BEING

Since a healthy body paves the way to a healthy mind, it was vital for me to fix my intellectual wellness, recognising that true fulfilment extended beyond occupational achievements. I dedicated time to self-reflection, engaging in activities that nourished my mind and soul. I resumed reading, started writing, and finding books on philosophy, psychology, and personal development. Reviving my hobbies, such as drawing, which once was my childhood passion. I sought out opportunities to sharpen my skills, attending art workshops, taking online courses, and engaging in meaningful conversations with the people I admire. These experiences broadened my horizon, reignited my curiosity, and helped me reconnect with my passions and interests which helped me to quiet the incessant chatter of my mind and to appreciate the present moment.

3-OCCUPATIONAL WELL-BEING

Clearly, I had consumed my past life to the extreme of this dimension which was once the centre of my life and my only focus. I began to evaluate my whole work aspects seeking all resources to learn how to optimise my workload and setting firm boundaries between work and personal life. I made a conscious effort to disconnect from work after hours and spent more time improving my work habits in a more efficient way. I silenced my work notifications on my phone and resisted the urge to check emails after a certain hour, utilising time management tools, regulating my meetings, prioritising my tasks, focusing on high-impact activities, and practicing delegation whenever possible. I also scheduled regular breaks throughout the day to recharge and avoid burnout and furthered my knowledge with online courses about time management and workload management tools. These small actions helped me to better manage my work in an efficient way while delivering the desired business performance without affecting my work-life balance.

4-FAMILY WELL-BEING

Taking care of my physical, intellectual & occupational well-being was a key enabler to facilitate more time to actively engage with my family. I looked at my family in a different way, creating more space for them in my life, prioritising their needs which extended far beyond being their own sole source of income. I made a conscious effort to spend more regular quality time with my parents, wife, and kids. I actively participated in my children's school activities, attending family gatherings & events. I learned how to actively listen to their feelings, dreams, and aspirations, offering guidance and support without imposing my own expectations. These experiences deepened my connection with my family, reminding me of the true meaning of happiness – love, joy, and the precious moments shared with those I cherish the most, my evenings and weekends became sacred spaces to reconnect together while reminding myself that what I am doing is eventually to facilitate a better life for us.

5-SOCIAL WELL-BEING

Gradually, I began to feel the change which encouraged me to extend my attention to my social well-being. I discovered the importance of the human connection element in my life, the value of networking & reconnecting with my loved ones and the joy of human interaction. I started to nurture my social life, reconnecting with my relatives, friends & colleagues whom I unintentionally disconnected from during my relentless pursuit of success. Interestingly I found out there are many of my work colleagues who I never tried to connect with them apart from business talks. I began to mark birthdays in my calendar, scheduling regular phone calls with them, planning weekend outings, organising day brunches, being present in gatherings and joining networking events & workshops. I rediscovered the joy of human connection, networking & the laughter shared with people around me and the comfort of genuine companionship.

6-FINANCIAL WELL-BEING

If I may say, financial illiteracy is a pandemic that has infected our societies. I overlooked managing my own financial wellness while focusing on my profession. I read once that many people don't possess enough knowledge of financial systems to make good choices that take care of their financial wellbeing. That left us dependent on a single income, forcing us to keep running in our own hamster wheel, waiting for the next pay cheque at the end of the month. You may not be surprised if I told you that I was measuring success & happiness with how wealthy people are. As a common person, I was easily bedazzled by the power of money as a tool for long-lasting happiness. That distracted me along the way, pushing me to always do more, work harder, and get promoted to reach a better financial status. In fact, the truth is not in how much income we can earn but how we can manage it well to reach financial freedom.

I started taking online courses about financial literacy, optimised my financial needs, carefully reviewed my expenses, and identified areas where I could cut back without sacrificing the quality of my life. I learned the difference between what I need vs. what I want. I embraced experiences over material possessions. This shift in perspective allowed me to reduce my reliance on material possessions and find contentment in simpler pleasures.

7-SPIRITUAL WELL-BEING

I consider my spiritual well-being to be the governance of all seven dimensions, gradually as I started to reconnect with my spiritual life, nurturing it and deepening my faith. Being a Muslim, I rededicated myself to my daily prayers, finding solace and guidance in the Quran and the peaceful teachings of Islam. I engaged in acts of charity, volunteering my time to help those in need, and seeking opportunities to serve my community. I also explored the teachings on mindfulness, gratitude, and finding contentment in the present moment. These practices helped me to cultivate a sense of inner peace, and reduced stress, providing me with a renewed direction. I also reconnected with nature, spending time outdoors, practicing meditation, disconnecting from my digital screens, and allowing myself to appreciate the beauty of the natural world. These practices helped me to cultivate a sense of inner peace and reconnect with my true self.

Looking back, I realised that true success is not to excel in one dimension but in cultivating a life of balance and fulfilment across all the seven dimensions of well-being. This newfound balance has brought me a sense of harmony that I never experienced.

Finally, I encourage you to take some time for reflection, asking yourself if you are living a balanced life that truly brings you joy and fulfilment. If you feel trapped & exhausted, this might be a sign of a change to embark on your own journey of self-discovery.

ABOUT THE AUTHOR

Ahmed Abdelaziz is a seasoned management professional with nearly two decades of experience in the automotive industry. Following his BSc. degree in Engineering he furthered his education with post-graduate studies in Project Management, Business Consulting, Influential Leadership, NLP, Business Psychology, and Organisational Behaviour. He successfully spearheaded several strategic initiatives, driving profitable business growth, and enhancing customer experience within leading automotive OEMs and dealerships across the Middle East region.

Amidst his professional achievements, he embarked on a journey of personal self-discovery that made him realise the true meaning of success that led him to a renewed purpose of his life to empower individuals unlock their full potential, help them live a balanced life of profound meaning with self-compassion. Drawing upon his leadership expertise and a deep understanding of human behaviour, he found his passion in guiding individuals on their transformative journeys of self-discovery achieving personal and professional success while cultivating a balanced lifestyle.

YOU CAN CONNECT WITH AHMED AT:

LinkedIn: *https://www.linkedin.com/in/ahmed-homepage*
Email: *ahmed.storyteller1@gmail.com*

Story Five

BREAKING BARRIERS

A Story of Bold Moves and Lasting Achievement.

THE JOURNEY BEGINS: DISCOVERING MY BEST SELF

Imagine waking up each morning with a burning desire to live your best life, confident that every day brings you closer to your dreams. This is the heart of my journey - a story of embracing change, overcoming obstacles, and unlocking immense potential. The moment I chose to take control of my life, everything began to transform. Each day became a step toward becoming the best version of myself.

A PERSONAL TURNING POINT

From a young age, I followed the traditional path to success: work hard, secure a stable job, and climb the corporate ladder. For years, I built what many would call a successful career. Yet, deep down, I felt there had to be more to life than the daily grind.

Then, everything changed when I met a visionary in the field of human potential and growth. He challenged me to visualise my ideal future without any limitations. This exercise was initially difficult, as my mind was trapped within the constraints of my current reality. But with his guidance, I broke free from these mental shackles. He taught me that success is not just about hard work – it is about cultivating the right mindset. This revelation marked the beginning of my transformative journey.

THE HEART OF MY STRUGGLES: FACING FAILURES, ENDS, AND REJECTIONS

Standing at the crossroads of my life, I often reflect on my corporate days. My journey began in 1997 as an Advocate & Solicitor of the High Court of Malaya, eventually becoming a dual-qualified Solicitor and Barrister of England and Wales. For fifteen years, a prestigious international firm in London was my professional playground. Yet, despite my success, an unquenchable desire for more lingered within me.

Leaving the familiar terrain of a corporate career for the uncharted waters of entrepreneurship was a leap of faith, filled with uncertainties. My initial ventures were riddled with failures and sleepless nights filled with self-doubt.

• FAIL = FIRST ATTEMPT IN LEARNING

I came to understand that 'Fail' stands for 'First Attempt In Learning.' Each setback was not a defeat but a stepping stone towards mastery. Failures teach resilience, patience, and innovation. Every time I fell, I rose stronger, armed with new insights and strategies. By embracing failures as learning opportunities, I navigated the turbulent tides of entrepreneurship.

• END = EFFORT NEVER DIES

One profound lesson I learned is that 'End' stands for 'Effort Never Dies.' Leaving my corporate career felt like the end - a chapter closing. But it was merely the beginning of a new journey, filled with fresh opportunities and challenges.

Each venture that concluded paved the way for new beginnings. This shift in perspective transformed my business approach. I no longer feared the end of a venture; I embraced it as a gateway to new possibilities.

• NO = NEXT OPPORTUNITY

The world of entrepreneurship is full of rejections. I learned to see 'No' as 'Next Opportunity.' Each rejection was a redirection, steering me towards more promising avenues.

The countless 'no's I encountered were detours leading me closer to where I needed to be. They taught me perseverance, adaptability, and the importance of relentless pursuit. Rejections became powerful motivators, challenging me to refine my approach and seek better opportunities.

NAVIGATING THE COMPLEXITIES

As I navigated the complexities of my business, these lessons - Fail as First Attempt In Learning, End as Effort Never Dies, and No as Next Opportunity - became my unwavering guiding principles. They reshaped my understanding of success and failure, transforming obstacles into opportunities for growth.

One of the most challenging moments came when a major venture I had been counting on fell through. It was a devastating blow, and I spent days questioning my decisions. However, I recalled my guide's wisdom and reframed this setback as a learning opportunity. I took a hard look at my business strategy, pinpointed the gaps, and turned to my mentors for their invaluable insights. This reflection and refinement process not only improved my business model but also fortified my resilience.

Faced with yet another rejection, I made the bold choice to completely pivot my strategy. This decisive action led to my first major breakthrough, proving the extraordinary power of adaptability and a growth mindset.

My transition from the corporate world to the world of entrepreneurship was not a solitary journey. It was a collective effort, supported by mentors, family, colleagues, and an unwavering belief in myself. A trusted guide and leader in personal success profoundly shaped my journey.

Looking back on my journey, I am filled with gratitude. Every struggle, failure, and rejection was a crucial stepping stone in my growth, teaching me to see challenges as opportunities for learning and advancement.

EMBRACING FAILURES, ENDS, AND REJECTIONS

To those facing failures, ends, and rejections, I urge you to embrace them. Redefine them as gateways to growth and success. Remember, 'Fail' stands for First Attempt In Learning, 'End' means Effort Never Dies, and 'No' is simply the Next Opportunity. Let these principles guide you as you navigate the complexities of your careers and lives.

In today's ever-changing and unpredictable world, resilience is your greatest ally. Embrace each setback as a setup for a comeback, and view every end as the dawn of a new beginning. Let every rejection propel you closer to your goals. With determination and relentless pursuit of your dreams, you can transcend any limit and achieve lasting success. If I can do it, so can you!

Remember: Your story is unique. Your potential is boundless. Your journey is just beginning. Take a leap of faith and watch your life transform in ways you never imagined. The power to create your dream life is in your hands. So, go out there and make it happen! Your future is a blank canvas waiting for your contribution.

GUIDED TO GREATNESS: THE IMPACT OF MINDSET AND MENTORSHIP

• FROM FEAR TO FAITH

Let me take you back to the moment that changed everything. I was at a crossroads, struggling with the decision to leave my secure job and pursue my dreams. The fear of the unknown was paralysing, but I knew I had to make a change. That's when I decided to invest in myself and seek guidance from an authority in human potential and growth.

• THE POWER OF MINDSET

The teachings of my esteemed guide were a revelation. He emphasised that Success is 95% Mindset and only 5% Strategy. This simple yet profound concept completely shifted my perspective. I realised that my limiting beliefs, not my circumstances, were the real barriers to my success.

• VISUALISING MY WISH FULFILLED

I immersed myself in the study of mindset, learning to harness the power of thinking from the results I desired and visualising my success as a done deal. My respected advisor taught me that our thoughts shape our reality, and by changing our thinking, we can transform our lives. This newfound understanding propelled me to take bold steps towards my goals.

• SETTING A BOLD GOAL

One of the most significant lessons I learned was the importance of setting a goal I had never pursued before - one that excited and scared me simultaneously. My trusted mentor guided me through a 90-day scientific process, helping me craft a strategic game plan to achieve my dreams. With this roadmap in hand, I took a quantum leap and started my own training and consulting business.

• EMBRACING CHALLENGES

The journey was far from easy. There were moments of doubt, fear, and uncertainty. Yet, I learned to embrace these challenges as opportunities for growth. Each setback became a stepping stone, teaching me valuable lessons and strengthening my resolve.

• AWAKENING TO SUCCESS

Through inspired daily disciplines and unwavering belief in myself, I began to see remarkable changes. My business took off, and I achieved milestones that once seemed impossible. More importantly, I experienced a profound shift in my personal life. I became more confident, resilient, and aligned with my true purpose and passion for helping others achieve this awakening.

One of the most memorable milestones was securing my first major client. This achievement was not just about the business; it was a validation of my journey and the principles I had embraced. It reinforced my belief in the power of mindset and persistence.

TAKE THE LEAP: IT IS YOUR TURN TO TAKE CHARGE

Now, I want to share the key steps that can help transform your life, just as they did for me. These steps are rooted in the solid scientific principles I gained from my guide and are designed to empower you to realise your potential and achieve your aspirations.

1. CULTIVATE A SUCCESS-DRIVEN MINDSET

Recognise that your thoughts shape your reality. Embrace the power of thinking from the perspective of your wish fulfilled, rather than your current circumstances. Believe in your ability to achieve great things. Replace self-doubt with self-belief and focus on what you can achieve right now.

2. SET A GOAL YOU HAVE NEVER PURSUED BEFORE

Take the time to define what you truly want in life, not just what you need to get by. Create a game plan with the help of a mentor, incorporate value-driven actions, adopt key daily disciplines for success, and continuously reflect, refine, and repeat the process.

3. SEEK MENTORSHIP

Surround yourself with like-minded individuals who empower you. Seek guidance from mentors who have walked the path you aspire to take. Learn from their experiences and integrate their insights into your own journey.

4. EMBRACE CHANGE

Change is inevitable, but personal growth is a choice. Don't hesitate to leave your comfort zone; the best things in life lie beyond it. Change can be daunting, but it is often the catalyst for growth. Seize new opportunities and be open to taking risks. The best investment you can make is in yourself, and it carries no risk.

5. TAKE INSPIRED ACTIONS

Success doesn't happen overnight, but it is within reach. It requires consistency and perseverance. Stay dedicated to your goals and take consistent actions, no matter how small, to move closer to your dreams. Remember, the path may change, but your goal remains until you achieve it.

6. REFLECT, REFINE AND REPEAT

Regularly evaluate your progress and adjust your approach as needed. Celebrate your successes, no matter how small, and learn from your setbacks. Continuously strive to improve and repeat this process.

7. STAY POSITIVE AND RESILIENT

Maintain a positive attitude, even when faced with challenges. Develop resilience and see setbacks as opportunities to learn and grow. Keep moving forward with determination and optimism, knowing that success is your birthright. If others can achieve it, so can you!

THE JOURNEY CONTINUES: GUIDING OTHERS TO THEIR BEST SELF

As I reflect on my journey, I am filled with immense gratitude for the path that has brought me here. I am passionate about sharing my story and the lessons I have learned to help others unlock their infinite potential and achieve their wildest dreams.

Remember, success leaves clues. By following a proven path and adopting the right mindset, you can achieve extraordinary results and make a real impact. My journey is a testament to the power of belief, perseverance, and the willingness to embrace change.

I invite you to reflect on your own journey:

- What are your dreams?
- What is holding you back?
- What steps can you take TODAY to move closer to your dreams?

The only limits that exist are the ones you place on yourself. Your future is a blank canvas, waiting for you to create your own narrative of success.

Let's embark on this journey of self-discovery and impactful transformation together. Believe in yourself, take inspired actions, and unleash the prosperous you within. Your dreams are within reach - pursue them with determination. Every step you take brings you closer to the life you envision. Stay focused, surround yourself with positive influences, and remember to celebrate every milestone. I will leave you with my favourite quote:

See the invisible, believe in the incredible, and receive what the masses would call impossible!

ABOUT THE AUTHOR

Kalpana Chandran had a secured corporate career - until one question changed everything: Is this all there is? That single thought sparked a bold transformation. Leaving behind certainty, she embraced the unknown, guided by faith, resilience, and the conviction that breakthroughs begin where comfort ends.

Today, as the founder of Quantum Leapers and a Proctor Gallagher Institute-certified consultant, Kalpana helps individuals, teams, and leaders break through mental barriers, master the science of mindset, and lead with agility in an era of disruption. She combines science-driven strategies with real-world application to create lasting transformation.

Recognised in Successful People in Malaysia & Singapore (2023) and honoured as a Global Woman of Influence for her contribution (2024), she is proof that reinvention is always possible. Through her work, she champions women, leaders, and changemakers to challenge the status quo, unlock their full potential, and shape the future - one bold decision at a time.

YOU CAN CONNECT WITH KALPANA AT:

LinkedIn: *https://www.linkedin.com/in/kalpanachandran168/*
Website: *https://www.quantum-leapers.com*
Email: *kalpana@quantum-leapers.com*

Story Six

ELEVATED MINDSET

Reclaiming Strength and Identity Through Healing.

I sat outside the conference room, a knot of humiliation tightening in my stomach. Dejected, I felt glued to the chair, replaying the scene in my mind. *What had I done to deserve this?* Being asked to leave a board meeting of a non-profit, I had been brought in to advise—the sting of it was relentless, a constant throb of pain. The wound festered, impacting my days and nights. I knew I needed help, but where to turn?

My journey took me from the supportive embrace of my family—growing up with three strong sisters and encouraging parents—to the high-pressure world of leading my first team at age 23 at the World Bank, surrounded by brilliant economists. This experience fuelled my desire to lead and coach, to stand in my authenticity and to empower others to achieve success, even without direct authority. I embraced the challenge of leadership coaching within the nonprofit sector, driven by a genuine desire to make a difference.

But this… this was different.

The humiliation I experienced at that board meeting wasn't an isolated incident. It was part of a pattern, a subtle erosion of my confidence and self-worth as I was being gaslighted.

With discipline and passion to contribute, I would give my 200% and achieve success in meeting the set objectives of any project I would be involved with, often to the annoyance of colleagues. In the end, they would have liked to take all of the credits. I found myself constantly second-guessing my actions, searching for ways to improve, yet always falling short. Frustration mounted, leading to self-doubt. *"Maybe there's something wrong with me,"* I whispered to myself, the insidious seed of doubt taking root.

Looking back, I understand the dynamics at play. My contributions, my very competence, were perceived as a threat by someone with a narcissistic personality. Their low self-esteem fuelled a need to diminish me, to push me down so they could appear superior. And the most insidious part? It was all done in private. In public, this individual was charming and charismatic—the epitome of a caring leader. This duality made it nearly impossible to share my experience and explain the subtle yet devastating manipulation I was enduring.

Who would believe me? This person was a master of image management, cultivating a carefully crafted public persona while wreaking havoc behind the scenes.

This is the insidious nature of narcissistic abuse.

It leaves the victim confused, questioning their own sanity. They ruminate endlessly, trying to understand what they did wrong and what lesson they need to learn. But there is no lesson to learn. There is nothing wrong with the victim. Their competence, their very presence, triggers the narcissist's deep-seated insecurities. Narcissistic abuse isn't just emotionally damaging; it can have profound and lasting effects on an individual's physical and mental health. The constant stress, manipulation, and self-doubt can manifest in a variety of ways.

THE DEVASTATING IMPACT OF NARCISSISTIC ABUSE ON HEALTH:

- **Mental Health**: Narcissistic abuse is a significant risk factor for developing depression, anxiety, and even post-traumatic stress disorder (PTSD). The constant invalidation, criticism, and manipulation can lead to feelings of hopelessness, worthlessness, and despair. The victim may experience flashbacks, nightmares, and hypervigilance, similar to those who have experienced other forms of trauma. Gaslighting can lead to a distorted sense of reality, making it difficult to trust one's own perceptions and judgments. This can result in increased anxiety and a constant state of unease and confusion.
- **Physical Health:** The chronic stress associated with narcissistic abuse can take a toll on the body. It can weaken the immune system, making the individual more susceptible to illness. It can also contribute to digestive problems, headaches, and other physical ailments. The constant state of "fight or flight" can lead to exhaustion, sleep disturbances, and even cardiovascular problems. In some cases, individuals may develop psychosomatic symptoms, where psychological distress manifests as physical pain or discomfort.
- **Emotional Dysregulation:** Narcissistic abuse can disrupt the ability to regulate emotions. Victims may experience intense mood swings, from extreme sadness and anger to feelings of numbness and detachment. They may struggle to manage their emotions in healthy ways, leading to further problems in their personal and professional lives. The con-

stant emotional rollercoaster can be exhausting and destabilising.

- **Cognitive Issues:** Constant stress and emotional turmoil can impair cognitive function. Victims may find it difficult to concentrate, remember things, and make decisions. Gaslighting can also affect their ability to think clearly and logically, as they constantly question their own perceptions. This can impact their performance at work or school and contribute to feelings of frustration and inadequacy.
- **Relationship Problems:** Narcissistic abuse can make it difficult to form and maintain healthy relationships. Victims may struggle with trust, intimacy, and boundaries. They may be drawn to other toxic relationships, repeating the pattern of abuse. The damage to their self-esteem and sense of self-worth can make them vulnerable to further exploitation. They hold back from sharing with the fear of being judged.

My purpose in sharing this story is twofold: First, *to raise awareness*. If you're experiencing something similar—whether at work or at home—you may not even realise you're a victim of narcissistic abuse. You might just feel confused, lost, and constantly doubting yourself. Please seek help. Don't wait until you crumble or until it's too late. Second, I hope this story serves as a mirror for those who may be engaging in these behaviours, even unknowingly, allowing them to see the profound trauma they inflict.

My journey to healing was long and arduous. As a coach, I naturally sought answers, talking to other coaches and counselors, but nothing seemed to resonate. I immersed myself in learning various modalities of human behaviour, including psychological behaviour changes, conversational intelligence, NLP, neuroscience, and energy modalities like Reiki. I became a Qi Gong Master to deepen my understanding of energy work. I explored the principles of positive psychology, attended courses, devoured books, and mastered how to best integrate these diverse tools to create lasting change, lead with confidence, and make a real impact.

One Sunday morning, while having coffee with my daughter, she offered a simple yet profound suggestion: "Mom, you're an accomplished coach. Why don't you coach yourself?" That was the turning point. I began to look inward, dissect my experiences, and understand the dynamics at play. This journey of self-discovery led me down a path of intensive understanding. And then I discovered it: Narcissistic Personality Disorder (NPD). The pieces of the puzzle clicked into place. I finally understood what I had been through. More importantly, I learned how to navigate these difficult situations, how to protect myself, and how to heal.

This understanding became crucial even in professional settings. Despite my experience and contributions, I was barred from a team meeting. The reason quietly whispered to me by the chairperson was: "my energy". The irony wasn't lost on me. This was the same person who had previously invited me to a leadership position within the organisation.

I recognised the familiar sting of insecurity and chose to disengage, refusing to let it derail me.

This incident, along with others like it, fuelled my determination to make a real difference. Despite the challenges, my leadership within a professional organisation proved to be a pivotal period. We inherited an organisation with limited engagement and a lack of representation. My team and I implemented a three-pillar strategy: focusing on member engagement, strengthening operations, and generating opportunities for our members.

We launched initiatives to connect with members, created communities for engagement, growth and collaboration, and streamlined operations for greater efficiency. Critically, we focused on generating business for our members by educating key stakeholders about the benefits of our services and actively participating in industry events. This led to a significant increase in demand, and our membership grew substantially. This success wasn't just about numbers; it was about creating a vibrant, supportive community. It was about elevating the coaching profession and ensuring its recognition by key stakeholders. We achieved greater representation within the organisation, establishing partnerships with key organisations. The processes we developed were even shared as a model for others.

In finding ways to overcome the challenges, I feel blessed to have learned several valuable lessons. Personally, this journey has been incredibly rewarding. I feel grateful for the opportunities as I continue to contribute and serve as a board of director. My experiences, both challenging and triumphant, have shaped me into the leader I am today. They have taught me the importance of resilience, self-awareness, and the unwavering belief in my own worth. These experiences have solidified my commitment to helping others navigate the complexities of narcissistic abuse and find their own voice—shaken but not stirred. My business model evolved to "Elevate Your Leadership: From Knowing to Owning Your Leadership." My chapter "Elevated Mindset" is based on my experiences to overcome leadership challenges.

Closer to home, I've felt blessed to be recognised for my contributions to the coaching field. I was recently named the Best Executive Coach in Singapore, the Top Coaching Voice on LinkedIn, and one of the Best 100 Coaches, along with Marshall Goldsmith.

Today, I use my experience and knowledge to help others who are trapped in the same cycle of abuse. Clients come to me confused and self-blaming, struggling to understand their difficult work or home situations. I help them see the reality of their circumstances, recognise the signs of being bullied, and develop strategies for coping and healing.

One recent client, a respected leader in his organisation, was being systematically undermined by his boss. Despite his best efforts, he could never seem to please him. The stress was so intense that his blood pressure had skyrocketed, requiring medication. Through coaching, I helped him understand the dynamics of the situation and develop new ways of responding. Within a month, his blood pressure returned to normal, and he was able to discontinue his medication. This is the power of understanding the mind, the neuroscience behind behaviour, and the transformative power of coaching.

If you recognise yourself in this story, please know that you are not alone. It's okay to seek help. It's okay to admit that you're struggling. It's okay to prioritise your own well-being. Others may not understand. They may doubt you, as my own friends and family did, often blinded by the carefully constructed facade of the narcissist. Society often pressures us to maintain a "perfect" image, to be "nice," even at the expense of our own well-being. This can make it incredibly difficult to recognise, let alone escape, abusive situations. In trying to appease others, we can lose sight of ourselves.

You might be tempted to learn about NPD and try to navigate this on your own, to be the "lone warrior." While self-education is valuable, embarking on this journey alone can be incredibly taxing and lead to burnout. I strongly encourage you to seek professional help. Just ensure you find a professional who understands you and has not only learned about it in theory. I struggled to find professional help for a long time, making this a crucial part of the healing journey.

It seems that I have found my life purpose in using my experience to coach others, helping them understand the dynamics of narcissistic abuse, develop coping mechanisms, and reclaim their lives. I help them see that they are not alone, that healing is possible, and that they can emerge from these experiences stronger and more resilient than ever before.

If you're facing a difficult situation at work, or if you constantly find yourself beating yourself up, ask yourself: Could I be a victim? Understanding the dynamics of bullying and narcissistic abuse is the first step toward healing and reclaiming your life. I'm here to help.

ABOUT THE AUTHOR

Jass Malaney is a distinguished recipient of the Prime Minister's Award in 2002 for the Reminder Service and has been honoured as the Best Executive Coach in Singapore, as well as being named one of the Best 100 Coaches Globally.

As a Strategic Consultant and C-level Coach, she specialises in helping organisations identify their needs and design effective people development solutions that drive impactful change for both individuals and the organisation.

With extensive global experience, Jass partners with key decision-makers and C-suite leaders, elevating their thinking and mindset to foster transformative change. She creates a supportive environment that encourages clients to explore their vision, values, and goals with clarity.

As a Team Coach, Jass is dedicated to building high-performing teams rooted in shared goals, values, teamwork, and accountability. As a Life Coach, she is passionate about helping clients achieve balance and fulfilment by blending emotional intelligence, executive presence, and transformative conversations.

YOU CAN CONNECT WITH JASS AT:

LinkedIn: *https://www.linkedin.com/in/executivecoachjassmalaney/*
Website: *https://jassmalaney.com/*
Instagram: *https://www.instagram.com/coachjassmalaney/*

Story Seven

EMBRACING PASSION

The Transformative Power of Cultivating a Hobby.

At school, when I ranked 5th, I was elated. Surprisingly, my parents did not share the same enthusiasm - perhaps because I was 5th from the bottom.

I tried my best to convince my parents that a 54th rank in my class of 59 students was not that bad, citing that five students scored less than me and ranked 55 onwards! For me, that was an achievement of sorts and a self-belief that I was 'still in the race'!

A pervasive sense of inadequacy marked my early academic experiences. Consistently ranking near the bottom of my class instilled a deep-seated lack of confidence. While I attempted to rationalise my performance, the societal pressure to excel, coupled with parental expectations, significantly eroded my self-esteem. This period fostered a forced introversion, profoundly impacting my formative years. I believe that these early experiences, or "conditioning," play a crucial role in shaping future achievements. For me, the absence of a "can-do" attitude and robust self-confidence presented a significant obstacle.

These were the early years of my childhood. Ranking amongst the top 10 is a matter of prestige. It's a societal issue, and I, too, faced it at home. Parental pressure to perform, peer group comparing my academic performance, and overall challenges of trying to cope with this pressure somehow took a toll on my confidence level. At times, it was unnerving, to say the least. I found myself increasingly becoming an introvert, almost as if I were being forced into it.

But that one big breakthrough (and the first one) came when I was just 12, given an opportunity to speak on the microphone. It was a simple storytelling event in my building complex – the first-ever opportunity to speak on stage, the moment I had waited for.

I vividly remember thinking twice, thrice, or perhaps a hundred times whether I should register for that particular storytelling competition. My inner voice, at times, said 'No' and, at other times, pushed me and convinced me to 'go for the kill'.

Eventually, I went ahead and registered for the competition. That turned out to be the first step. Then came the actual moment when my name was announced, and I had to finally 'be there' on the stage. It was nervously magical. I didn't know whether I was nervous or if it was just unfolding without me realising what was happening. By the time I realised what was going on, I had already narrated the story, done and dusted!

Finally, the Golden Moment arrived- the prizes were announced. I was selected as the 'Best Storyteller' that evening. Upon hearing my name being announced, my feet sank in, but my confidence level shot up. That short distance from the chair where I was seated up to the dais to accept the prize felt nothing less than accepting an 'Oscar' sans the speech!

My relatives, who were watching me narrate the story, still pull my leg today, saying that I almost 'ate the mic' that day. But that particular evening, I felt 'accepted'; I felt that 'it's possible', and most importantly, it was a matter of pride not just for me but also for my parents. This 'storytelling' competition was just the beginning of what would later unfold as a hobby turning into a successful career.

My next opportunity to 'believe in myself' came when I received an invite for an audition for a newly launched FM channel in Mumbai. I reached the venue well in advance of the scheduled time only to find over 300 other candidates. These candidates were self-introducing to one another. Some of them had a background in film industry auditioning, whilst some were professional speakers, a few had tried their hand at animation or documentary voice overs. My claim to fame was – hosting my building complex's Annual Fancy Dress event, announcing 'Entry number 1- Joker'.

Listening to others talk about their media experiences, I felt an inferiority complex, and self-doubt started to creep in. Would I make it or not? Was it the right decision to be there? What if I didn't get selected? How would I face defeat? All kinds of negative thoughts started to swarm in my mind. My anxiety levels shot up tremendously. I could see the challenge ahead; it was not going to be easy, let alone a cakewalk. I started to lose confidence. But then something magical happened.

On my way from the railway station to the radio studio, I came across a large advertising hoarding of Mr Amitabh Bacchchan (a top-notch Indian film personality). The tagline read- 'Believe in yourself, Believe in the Best'. This tagline sparked and lifted my confidence levels. We were down to

15 candidates out of the 300+, and only five were selected. I was one of them! That day was my second booster- a shot of confidence. I felt I had arrived. I had just started pursuing a hobby, which went on to become a second career in life.

The five of us got an opportunity to meet the selection team once our in-studio training started. One of the seniors who selected me had very appreciative comments for all of us who were selected. She told me that all the 300+ were good at their script and the voice auditions. What separated us was our confidence levels. They had judged us based on how confidently we opened the studio door, walked up to the microphone, and delivered our voice test. That was all that mattered.

This was certainly a WOW moment in my life. From competing in a fancy dress competition with an audience of over 100, I had now graduated to being a radio jockey broadcasting to a base of a million listeners! Confidence levels reached new heights that day. I was 'on-air,' literally!

Due to COVID, I couldn't travel to India from Hong Kong, which led to the discontinuation of my radio career – a significant disappointment. I started contemplating my options and what next steps I could take to continue with my passion for 'speaking into the microphone'. And phew! The idea of starting a podcast originated. I started a business podcast titled 'The Sound of Money'. I looked forward to weekends when I would connect with my guests, record their interviews, edit the content, upload on YouTube, and share across social media

In the initial years, the response and feedback were slow but steady. There were 'down' moments when the views and likes did not increase. My inner voice often told me that a podcast won't work. I had to revisit my thoughts on 'self-belief'. A friend from the digital media world strongly advised me that 'patience, hard work, resilience, and consistency' was the key.

Four years later, my podcasting journey is now in a different orbit. With over 8 million impressions on social media, several episodes crossing the 100K views mark, and a lineup of top-notch guests, the podcasting journey has kicked off on a very different level. Yes, this is my 3rd booster shot of confidence level breaking barriers. I have learned many lessons from this journey, which is leading me toward not only success but also fulfillment.

Firstly, the importance of cultivating a hobby is underscored. A hobby, I believe, serves as a sculptor of one's personality, shaping and refining it over time. It provides a channel for self-expression and personal growth. It is a journey of endless capabilities.

Secondly, a hobby bolsters confidence levels. Engaging in activities one loves fosters positive character development, instilling a sense of achievement and self-assurance. I have experienced enough 'down' moments in life. Thirdly, my own experience as a Radio Jockey has taught me the virtue of perseverance. Life demands patience, and success is a gradual process. Hard work, coupled with patience, is the key to achieving one's goals, and this is a message I aim to impart clubbed with few learnings as a podcaster now. What started as an alternate career in the mid-90s took me a comfortable 25+ years to fructify into a successful podcasting career.

Furthermore, hobbies prepare you to accept and face challenges, embracing failures as opportunities for learning. By sharing my journey of overcoming rejections and setbacks, I believe such setbacks are stepping stones rather than stumbling blocks, emphasising the importance of resilience.

Lastly, the significance of having "pacers" in life is highlighted. Friends, family, and relatives can play pivotal roles as sources of encouragement and motivation, acting as pillars of support in the pursuit of objectives. Identifying and cherishing these influencers is crucial for personal and professional growth. In essence, hobbies play a vital role in one's transformative process and development, serving as supportive networks that propel individuals toward success.

One key learning: Given my childhood, which was often marked by low self-esteem and dejection, I believe that those days are equally important in one's life. They keep you grounded, make you strong, and, more importantly, help you empathise with someone who may be undergoing a similar situation.

In addressing 'The Power of a Hobby,' I believe it's crucial for my community, especially students and my audiences, to recognise that life isn't a one-shot victory; it's an ongoing journey. A hobby akin to a sweet dessert adds joy and anticipation to this journey. It is important to understand that amidst challenges, a hobby provides a refuge and contributes to personal growth. In a world focused on instant results, this idea encourages a more profound perspective, emphasising the enduring value of investing time in activities that bring joy and fulfillment.

In hindsight, my early failures were stepping stones to success. Life may have been challenging to manage, but failures can be great learning experiences. They helped me become strong and accept challenges that came along the way. Despite initial challenges and periods of self-doubt, I persevered, guided by the principles of patience, hard work, resilience, and consistency. This success represents a significant affirmation of my abilities.

Coming back to my academic story, it was not that bad after all! I had decent rankings all through my career- ended up earning a postgraduate MBA from a very prestigious institution in Mumbai. It was a deep sense of achievement, after all the brickbats of my early school career, this was my 4th booster shot of feeling that I had arrived in life! Reflecting on my early struggles with self-esteem, I recognise their inherent value. These experiences fostered empathy and provided a foundation for resilience. They instilled in me the understanding that setbacks are not definitive failures but rather opportunities for learning and growth.

Introspecting on each of these fun and not-so-fun moments, I realised that life throws numerous opportunities at you. In most cases, I accepted such opportunities, only to find that they simply barged in. It's up to you to accept or reject them.

In conclusion, the power of a hobby lies in its capacity to transform individuals. It is a continuous journey of self-discovery and personal development. A hobby provides a refuge during challenging times and contributes significantly to overall well-being. It reminds us that life is a multifaceted journey, and cultivating a passion provides a constant source of purpose and resilience.

My academic journey ultimately culminated in a postgraduate MBA from a prestigious institution, a testament to the fact that early struggles do not define future potential. Life presents numerous opportunities; it is our choice to embrace or reject them. By cultivating a hobby, we equip ourselves with the confidence, resilience, and purpose to navigate these opportunities and achieve fulfilling lives.

ABOUT THE AUTHOR

Santosh Sirur is a seasoned banking professional with over 25 years of experience. He holds an MBA from JBIMS and has held leadership positions in Hong Kong and India.

In addition to his banking career, he is also a podcaster, and his flagship business podcast, The Sound of Money, has received over 8 million impressions. With more than 25 years of experience as a broadcaster at All India Radio (FM), Santosh has co-authored the book 'AML Unplugged.' He has also been featured in "Secrets of the Engaging Warrior," a journey that inspires cross-cultural connections across Asia. Additionally, he was invited to speak at TEDx Hong Kong.

Santosh has worked as a soft skills coach and was recently invited to speak as the keynote speaker at the Amazing Goa event, where he addressed over 400 college students. He has also been invited to speak at various conventions, including ET Now Gurukul and India Factoring.

YOU CAN CONNECT WITH SANTOSH AT:

LinkedIn: *https://www.linkedin.com/in/santosh-sirur-143bb223/*

Podcast: *https://santoshsirur.com/podcast*

Email: *santoshsirur@rediffmail.com*

Story Eight

FINDING MY TRUE NORTH STAR

Driven by Purpose and Powered by People.

As I stood on the grand stage in Singapore, clutching the prestigious **Global Women of Influence Awards 2024**—the golden lady with wings—it felt like more than a trophy; it symbolised a profound journey of **owning my crown with pride while wearing it with humility**—a testament to the power of **hard work, positivity, and resilience.**

Growing up with two strong and determined sisters, and surrounded by male allies—friends, brothers, and classmates—instilled in me the belief that gender was never a barrier. My parents raised us to believe we were unstoppable and capable of achieving all of our dreams.

While I now revel in my role as a finance professional in tech, life first tested me early in my career when I failed my Chartered Accountancy exam. It was a crushing blow; I disappointed myself and my allies, causing overwhelming grief and self-doubt. I could not face my family for some weeks. However, through the pain, a pivotal choice emerged: to fight and surmount the odds. With careful strategy and effort, I passed the exam and then went on to achieve multiple other global finance qualifications. It's life's splendid irony that my first recognition was directly linked to my first critical failure! I received the Professional Women Achiever Award from the Institute of Chartered Accountants of India. As I addressed the latest batch of newly qualified accountants on my journey into tech, I looked at the room filled with over 1,000 accountants starting their careers and reiterated the first of **my five Personal Truths: failure is not the end—it's thc foundation for your next success.**

Stepping into the professional world of technology—then a male bastion often reserved for those with technical and engineering backgrounds—was a stark awakening. Challenging gender stereotypes meant standing up to the deeply ingrained **"Tribe Culture."** Additionally, Indian tech teams were often dismissed as a "back office," with no presence or say in high-stakes conversations.

I vividly remember an onsite project in Sweden, where I was deputed as team lead—the only woman and the youngest, often referred to as the under-19 team captain. In my first client meeting, an attendee commented that their IT experience surpassed my age. The implied scepticism fuelled my success in a project that most experienced peers in the industry feared to deliver. I have subsequently won and delivered many more complex finance projects—so that was the start of a journey to becoming a **torchbearer for change**. The scepticism I faced taught me to challenge stereotypes, question established norms, and confront cultural barriers, ageism, and sexism, while taking chances on people different from me.

There were moments of self-doubt—times when I questioned if I truly deserved my success. But each doubt became a catalyst, reminding me to rise, to push, and to believe. Every idea I championed, every boundary I broke, was proof that greatness doesn't come from avoiding challenges; it comes from facing them head-on. In those moments, I reminded the world that **true power lies not in dominance but in the courage to confront it.**

Starting as an accountant in India and transitioning into a technology lead in Singapore, I took the path less travelled. Along the way, I became committed to forging pathways for women in technology and finance. Now, as I hold the golden lady with her wings outstretched, I see more than an award. I see a beacon of hope—a symbol of what's possible when we dare to dream, believe in ourselves, and embrace the power within. For this isn't just about my journey; it's about the countless possibilities waiting for those brave enough to rise above, to persevere, and to redefine what's possible.

Life, as I've come to realise, is made bright by a multitude of joys and countless lessons. One of my most humbling moments and key lessons came when I missed out on a promotion I genuinely believed I deserved. The sting of disappointment was sharp when I did not see my name on the list. Being the fodder for office gossip cut even deeper.

Then came the remark that changed everything. A colleague, with blunt honesty, said, "Well, taking on this role was your personal choice, so you can't really complain." At that moment, I realised—this was my path. If I had chosen this journey, I had to own not just the rewards but also the setbacks and the lessons it offered. That statement catalysed my frustration into fuel. I revisited my goals, reflected on my strengths, and redefined what I truly wanted to achieve.

With a renewed sense of clarity, I decided to speak to a few leaders and take up a new leadership role where I would gain the right visibility. I stated my terms of engagement upfront and crafted a winning promotion strategy with the help of my close friends and colleagues. In time, I not only received my much-deserved promotion in my dream role, but it also became a stepping stone for my nomination for another Global Award and future opportunities.

When I reflected on why a lost promotion impacted me so much, I realised it was a superficial marker of success, following organisational and societal norms. I redefined my rules. This life lesson brought me **my second Personal Truth: success is not about climbing a ladder someone else built; it is about building your own path. My Game + My Rules = My Success.**

Five years ago, I arrived in Singapore, my heart racing with a mix of apprehension and hope. I was at the pinnacle of my career in India, and the decision to leave it all behind—to take a leap of faith into the unknown—felt like hitting the restart button on life. My forte lay in the airline, power, insurance, manufacturing, and other non-banking industries. That restart button helped me venture into banking and the financial industry—a completely foreign turf. I aced the learning game, garnering the support of some great leaders. They recognised my true potential and provided me with a psychologically safe ground to excel. Today, I thank my younger self for having the courage to take that risk—and for giving me the **freedom to fail.**

Sushmita Sen, the first Indian to win the Miss Universe title, once said in an interview, "I have no fear of failure." She embraced imperfection and recognised that failure is simply part of the law of averages. Her words resonate deeply with me. Here, I was introduced to **my third Personal Truth: acceptance of the possibility of failure frees the mind and opens the path to growth.**

Another milestone etched into my journey was when I embarked on my first mentorship program, leading a spirited team of six mentees. We called ourselves **SWAT**—Successful Women Achieving Together—a name that symbolised our shared dreams and strong bonds. Even a decade later, we still celebrate each other's victories—big and small. Recently, my heart swelled with pride when one of them shared her recognition for conducting a women's empowerment initiative at her workplace. In that moment, I saw the beauty of the ripple effect—how the lessons I had the privilege to learn from my leaders were being passed on by my mentees.

For the last few years, I have been working with a non-profit organisation, mentoring multiple individuals who are being reskilled to take up technology jobs from non-technology backgrounds. It was very fulfilling when, in my first batch, a lady from a finance background who had lost her job during the pandemic and was doing Grab food delivery got placed with a global technology company. Paying it forward always pays. Here is **my fourth Personal Truth: true success lies not only in climbing higher but in lifting others along the journey. Our Game + Our Rules = Our Success.**

In the grand tapestry of my journey, there are unsung heroes whose seemingly small actions leave a profound impact. I fondly remember one such knight from a critical project we undertook. He ensured our coffee reached our desks, bringing hot cheer during countless late nights. At our Project Go-Live speech, we gave him a heartfelt vote of thanks. His job might have seemed mundane and often thankless, but when his name echoed in the room, the genuine smile that lit up his face was a moment etched in my memory forever.

This project wasn't just a milestone in deliverables—it was a testament to the spirit of leadership and respect. Every team member's opinion was valued, and leaders went above and beyond, ensuring even the smallest concerns were addressed. One poignant example was the client leads personally ensuring that female team members reached home safely after late nights—a gesture that spoke volumes about the care and camaraderie within the team.

The cherry on top? This project was selected as a global success case study and showcased at a prestigious forum in the U.S. I still remember standing at the U.S. immigration desk when the officer, noticing my purpose of travel, asked, "You're here to present a case study to a global audience—are you nervous?" With a confident smile, I replied, "I'm so proud of what we achieved that there's simply no room for nervousness. This project was not just about deliverables or accolades—it was about building a culture of respect, teamwork, and unwavering pride in our shared accomplishments. It remains a shining example of what true leadership and collaboration can achieve."

Later in my journey, I was also fortunate to receive the support of a leader I deeply respect. They humbly addressed the team, reaffirming my belief in good leadership by saying, "I may not have all the answers to your challenges, but I promise to listen, support, and stand by you."

Here evolved **my fifth Personal Truth: True leadership is about embodying humility, wisdom, and compassion to inspire and guide others.**

Together, these five personal truths culminate in one universal understanding: our power as global women influencers comes not from striving for perfection but from living with purpose, persevering through challenges, and empowering others by staying true to ourselves. My story, though seemingly familiar—a woman juggling career, dreams, and family—was never mine alone. It is shaped by the silent heroes and sheroes: mentors, colleagues, friends, and family who supported me through every high and low.

My parents were my unwavering pillars of support, encouraging my dreams, while my sisters became my 3 a.m. confidantes, offering laughter and advice. My husband single-handedly cared for our infant while I navigated complex projects late into the night. A college professor transformed my view of tax, igniting my passion for chartered accountancy. In the workplace, mentors redefined strength, with one leader entrusting me with a high-stakes project others feared. This camaraderie forged lifelong friendships as teammates cooked meals when I skipped lunch. Airline crews added a touch of unity on long flights, and I proudly embraced the title "CFO's Best Friend" - given to me by my best friend.

These moments are more than just stories; they are snapshots of resilience, trust, and connection. Failures weren't roadblocks—they were chapters of a narrative I chose to rewrite. I embraced my imperfections, learning to love my flawed but authentic self. As I accepted the award that evening, I felt a surge of gratitude. This achievement wasn't mine alone; it belonged to everyone who believed in me, stood by me, taught me, and lifted me higher. It equally belonged to my greatest hero, my father, my guiding light, who taught me his life's mantra: "*Poochne mein kya hai*?" (What's the harm in asking?). He instilled in me the courage to ask for what I desired—by asking, we open doors that would otherwise remain closed.

My father, in his humility, always attributes his success to his shero: my mother. Together, they showed me that true influence lies in the lives we touch, the dreams we inspire, and the stories we dare to tell. So, I dedicate this journey to every person who walks beside me. This is not just my story—it's ours. Driven by purpose and powered by people, we rise together.

ABOUT THE AUTHOR

Netra Ranjan Prabhu is currently working as a Tech Lead with a global bank. Her journey from an accountant to working for global technology companies for over 18 years, and then moving to a global bank, has been an exciting one, taking a road less travelled and forging new pathways for women in finance and technology. She has extensive experience leading complex finance transformation projects across multiple industries, including telecom, power, insurance, airlines, and banking, with large global companies based in India, the U.S., Switzerland, Malaysia, Hong Kong, and Singapore, to name a few.

For her ground-breaking journey in the world of fintech, she won the Professional Woman Achiever Award in 2018 from the Institute of Chartered Accountants of India. In 2021, she was a finalist in the Channel Asia Women in ICT Awards in Singapore and in the Women in Tech Excellence Awards in the U.K. In 2024, she was recognised as the winner of the Global Women of Influence Awards in Singapore.

Netra is also very passionate about giving back to society and has been supporting a non-profit organisation in their endeavours.

YOU CAN CONNECT WITH NETRA AT:

LinkedIn: *https://www.linkedin.com/in/netraprabhu/*
Email: *npsingp10@gmail.com*

Story Nine

FROM BOARDROOMS TO BREAKFAST TABLES

The Balancing Act of a Lifetime.

INTRODUCTION: THE JUGGLING ACT

As I reflect on this journey through the lens of a woman's daily life, I realise just how often we navigate a delicate balance. One summer morning, my alarm rang, dragging me out of sleep. As I blinked my eyes open, the reality of the day set in. I had an important meeting where I was presenting my proposal to a room full of stakeholders, competing against another team. The stakes were high, and I was determined to win. I was ready, or so I thought.

Just as I started to prepare for the big day, my son walked in with a look of panic. He had forgotten to mention that his school project, due that very day, was still unfinished. My husband was travelling (usually my backup plan), and the maid had called in sick for the day (another backup plan gone). Cue the sense of impending doom.

My heart raced, and my mind spiralled—how could I be everywhere at once? I needed to be on time for work, but I also couldn't shake the guilt of letting my son down. Sound familiar? This chaotic balancing act is something many of us experience over and over. No matter how much we plan, life always seems to throw us a curveball. The truth is, no woman's life is a bed of roses. Even roses have their thorns.

"THE ART OF SAYING NO (WITHOUT GUILT)"

A "no" to an activity reinforces a "yes" to another activity. Yes and no are about priorities, not about people or events. It is an opportunity to communicate priorities and allocate resources to what is most important. One particular incident stands out, illustrating the delicate balance between professional commitments and personal priorities.

It was a day when a global leader was visiting India, and there were after-work drinks and dinner arrangements for the team. But that same evening, I had to attend my daughter's annual day. I attended the meetings during the day but politely declined the invitation to the evening event. For me, the joy of seeing my daughter's eyes searching for me in the audience and the priceless moment when I waved from the audience and smiled thereafter outweighed any other event. No woman needs to feel guilty for declining an office event to be at a special day for a child.

Never let guilt—whether self-imposed or pushed upon you by society—hold you back. Not your colleagues. Not your family. Not your friends. Not anyone.

"GLASS CEILINGS & STICKY FLOORS"

As women in the workplace, we often face many stereotypes and are easily labelled: "Too Soft, Too Tough." Women are expected to show empathy at work, but what do you do if you are an "Alpha female"?

I have always been driven and ambitious; normal is boring. I wanted to live with a purpose. I am very comfortable being with myself and embracing change, and I love working with people. I can enter a room full of strangers and still be comfortable having a conversation.

At one point, I was working in a leadership position at a very prestigious American investment bank. When the subprime crisis hit, the bank declared bankruptcy. I had just had my second child, who was only a year and a half old, and was managing a home loan. Everyone around me scrambled, interviewing for any job they could find. I decided to stay. When another renowned investment bank took over operations, I had an enriching experience for over a decade with the firm.

Then, an unexpected opportunity came knocking—a role that was completely out of my comfort zone, in a new city with a different firm. I pondered over it, evaluated it thoroughly, and ultimately took the leap of faith! When we face such opportunities, there is a lot of risk involved in moving out of our safety net. I can't say I didn't have my doubts, but always acknowledging the worst that can happen has made me confident to move ahead. Always have a Plan B!

Fast forward five years, I can confidently say it was one of the best decisions I ever made. My family also adapted and thrived.

A key learning: Sometimes, we hold ourselves back more than others do. The power is within! Take the risk! Go for it!

"CRASHING WITHOUT BURNING"

I love the image of an iceberg—you see the beauty of the surface and admire it. But how often do we stop to think about where its strength lies? Beneath the water, unseen, lies a massive foundation that holds it up. Similarly, when we see successful individuals, especially women, we are often in awe, wondering how they got there. But success is never without its share of struggles—heartburn, disappointments, and unexpected detours. Not everything goes according to plan, and that's okay.

There was a time in my life when I eagerly looked forward to a higher role that I wholeheartedly believed I deserved. But—you guessed it—I didn't get it. Almost a decade has passed, yet I still feel a twinge of pain when I think about it. But here's the thing: it happened at the right time. It was a wake-up call, and I moved on to my next big opportunity. I could have stayed, hoping that one day the role would be mine, but that's not who I am. I'm ambitious (and unapologetically so), and I chose to move forward. I often wonder how different my life would have been if I had stayed. Looking back, I now see that setback as one of the best things that ever happened to me. At the time, it felt like a crushing disappointment (and trust me, I'm understating it), but I bounced back and landed exactly where I wanted to be.

It's not about never failing or not getting what you desire—it's about what you do next. Do you break down and give up, or do you rise, shake off the dust, and push forward? Grit and resilience come from within. No matter how much encouragement you receive, the fire to keep going has to be yours.

There are good days and challenging days (I refuse to call them bad days for a reason). Staying positive and believing that everything happens for a reason has been my greatest teacher. Every experience has shaped me into a more confident person—both professionally and personally.

I see so many people around me who are unhappy, constantly complaining, and drowning in negativity. And if you're vulnerable, that energy is contagious. I have consciously chosen to be an optimist. I am still training myself not to overthink (work in progress!), and I've accepted that I can't control everything. I remind myself every day—I am not perfect.

But I do know this: the best is yet to come!

"INVISIBLE LABOUR: THE WORK NO ONE ACKNOWLEDGES"

Most mornings, before I even open my eyes, my thoughts are already racing: What needs to get done today? Planning my daughter's birthday, organising a surprise for her friends, ordering balloons, remembering that my maid mentioned we're out of groceries, scheduling the AC service—on and on it goes.

This silent mental load, the invisible labour that women carry—remembering birthdays, planning vacations, ensuring the home runs smoothly—is immeasurable. And it doesn't stop at home.

In corporate settings, this labour takes on a different form. Women are often expected to be the emotional anchors—mentoring, boosting team morale, carrying a reassuring smile (because even if you move past a bad day, your team might not recover as quickly), and showing up at events because the team expects to see you there. Organising town halls and ensuring engagement—it's only noticed when it's not done. The unspoken burden of these expectations falls disproportionately on women.

"FOCUSING ON WHAT TRULY MATTERS"

I learned one thing very early in life: the art of letting go. Don't do tasks that can be delegated. Someone who is an expert can do it better than you. Your time is precious.

Quoting an instance when we remodelled our house in Mumbai during COVID, I managed the entire project remotely from Bengaluru. I spent hours obsessing over the smallest details—not because I had to, but because I wanted to. I have an eye for this kind of work, and it was worth my time.

At work, my priority is decision-making. Over the years, I've noticed that even the best subject matter experts often struggle to make decisions. Why that happens is a discussion for another time! But that's where I add the most value—cutting through ambiguity and moving things forward.

I also dedicate a lot of time to mentoring and coaching—both men and women. Women, in particular, need more role models, yet there are so few. Making myself available is one of the best uses of my time—because only I can do that.

The only way to achieve peace of mind without being overwhelmed by expectations from life is to be intentional about where you spend your time. Once you delegate, trust that the job will get done. There's no point in micromanaging (trust me, it's a trap!).

The mental load will never fully disappear, but learning to let go is the first step to reclaiming your time—and your sanity.

"FROM OFFICE POLITICS TO FAMILY DIPLOMACY"

You get to choose your friends—but you don't get to choose your family. And sometimes, navigating corporate politics feels easier than managing family dynamics. In business, there are defined roles, clear incentives, and the option to walk away. With family? There's no exit strategy. So, we compromise, we adapt, and we learn that the best approach is simple: give respect to get respect.

CORPORATE LESSONS FOR PERSONAL RELATIONSHIPS

Being a corporate professional has taught me invaluable lessons that apply just as much to managing personal relationships as they do to leading teams.

- **Network to manage relationships** – Whether in business or family, staying connected is key. The effort you put into maintaining relationships determines the quality of those connections.
- **Set boundaries** – Just as we define professional boundaries at work, we need to do the same at home. Even with family, it's crucial to make it clear what's acceptable and what's not.

I recently came across a reel featuring Mel Robbins. She asked Viola Davis, "What relationship advice would you give your daughter?" Davis' answer struck a chord: "You are the love of your life." She explained that loving yourself—caring for your health, setting boundaries, and valuing your well-being—is the foundation of any relationship. If you don't take care of yourself, how can you show up for others?

Choose where you invest your energy wisely—because the most valuable relationship you have is the one with yourself.

CONCLUSION: SHAKEN, STIRRED, BUT STILL STANDING

Every day I live on this planet, I learn a new skill, gain knowledge, and discover what I should do and what I should say "no" to. Be it success in the corporate world, raising a family, or spending time with friends, I do it the way I like! It's truly shaped me into the woman and leader I am today!

Life has a way of shaking us, stirring us, and, at times, testing our resilience in ways we never anticipated and never knew we could. Through the highs and lows of life, I have learned that the key is not to avoid storms, but rather to ride the tide in your stride!

Each experience I have gained—whether as a leader, mother, wife, or daughter—has added a new layer of understanding, reinforcing the belief that success is not about having a perfect life, but about embracing its imperfections with confidence and owning it!

Challenges will come that we can't control, but they don't define us—our response to them does!

As you turn this final page of my story, I hope you carry with you a reminder that setbacks are not roadblocks; they are stepping stones. True strength lies in staying undeterred.

Keep learning, keep evolving, keep moving!

ABOUT THE AUTHOR

Padma Priya Saraswatula (Priya) is a trailblazing leader with close to three decades of corporate experience, mastering the art of balancing high-stakes executive roles with the responsibilities of a deeply rooted personal life. She is celebrated for her transformative leadership and unwavering commitment to excellence.

In 2024, she was honoured with the Corporate Leadership Award by IWAA and recognised as one of the 'Top 10 Women Leaders' by JobsForHer (HerKey) in both 2022 and 2023. Additionally, she received the Herrising Award and was named among the 'Top 20 DivHERsity Champions (SMEs/Startups)' by HerKey in 2023 and 2024.

In her chapter, Priya distills powerful, hard-earned lessons from her journey as a daughter, wife, and mother, sharing valuable insights on resilience, leadership, and finding harmony across life's diverse roles. With sharp insights and heartfelt reflections, she inspires readers to embrace resilience, thrive under pressure, and find harmony in both their professional and personal lives.

YOU CAN CONNECT WITH PRIYA ON:

LinkedIn: *http://linkedin.com/in/padma-priya-saraswatula-1115a0a*
Instagram: *https://www.instagram.com/priyastravelogue*
Email: *contactpadmapriya@gmail.com*

Story Ten

FROM FAMILY STRUGGLES TO PROFESSIONAL SUCCESS

Lessons Learnt About Resilience & Perseverance.

A HUMBLE BEGINNING IN PENANG

My story begins in the heart of Penang, Malaysia—a place known for its mix of traditional charm and modern energy. I was born and raised in a small urban town on the island, where the pace of life was slower and more intimate. As an only child, my early years were marked by the loving, if somewhat distant, care of my parents, both of whom were busy with their careers. While they provided for me materially, the emotional support that every child craves was more often given to me by my grandmother, a resilient woman who played a central role in my upbringing.

My grandmother's house was my source of comfort and security, a sanctuary that shielded me from the stresses of my parents' professional lives. Here, I learned important life lessons about hard work, respect, and empathy. The house was filled with the aroma of freshly cooked meals, laughter, and stories of the past—stories that shaped my understanding of resilience and the value of community.

Despite my grandmother's stability, I couldn't ignore the growing emotional distance between my parents. I longed for the closeness I saw in other families, yet I struggled to find the words to fully express or understand the gap that had formed.

THE SEPARATION OF HER PARENTS: A DEFINING MOMENT

At the age of 16, my world changed forever. My parents separated, a decision that felt sudden and painful. Although I had sensed tensions between them, the finality of the divorce hit me hard. It shattered the idealised image I had of my family, leaving me overwhelmed with confusion and loss.

In the wake of the separation, I was thrust into an emotional adult role, helping both my mother and father navigate the fallout. My mother, deeply hurt by the end of her marriage, leaned heavily on me for emotional support, sharing her worries and sadness. On the other hand, my father, while still present in my life, became more withdrawn and distant. I found myself caught between two worlds, often torn between my loyalty to both parents and the desire to shield myself from their pain.

Amid this chaos, I found solace in my schoolwork and the stability of my grandmother's home. During the early days of my parents' separation, I found myself swamped in a sea of conflicting emotions. A child's mind, so often malleable and impressionable, struggled to comprehend the reality of fractured family dynamics. Yet, my grandmother possessed an extraordinary gift for offering comfort without judgment. She witnessed my silent tears and heavy sighs, and instead of forcing conversation about the situation that consumed much of my thoughts, she provided an atmosphere of unwavering support. Her nurturing presence was the anchor I didn't know I needed. Yet, even her presence couldn't fully erase the emotional turmoil I experienced as a result of the divorce.

However, it was remarkable how the adolescence I spent under my grandmother's influence shaped my identity. In the years that followed, as I transitioned into adulthood, her teachings guided my steps. As I faced my own challenges, be it academic or personal, I carried her spirit with me; her gentle nudges toward optimism intertwined seamlessly with my actions. In a time when the world felt insurmountably daunting, her perspective had endowed me with a lens of hope.

A PATH IN ECONOMICS: THE LOVE FOR NUMBERS

Though my personal life was turbulent, I threw myself into my studies, particularly focusing on mathematics and economics. I had always excelled in subjects that required logical thinking and problem-solving, and I found that economics provided the perfect outlet for these strengths. Unlike many of my peers who were drawn to more creative or artistic pursuits, I found fulfilment in the structured world of numbers, markets, and economic theory. In economics, I discovered a sense of order—a realm where data and trends tell a coherent story.

My interest in economics was fuelled by a desire to understand the world around me. I was fascinated by how markets operated, how nations made economic decisions, and how individuals and businesses interact within the economy. As I delved deeper into my studies, my passion grew; I learned to analyse complex financial systems, make predictions, and apply mathematical models to real-world problems. I excelled in my classes, winning awards and recognition from professors for my sharp analytical mind and my ability to see patterns that others missed.

I was convinced that the analytical skills I cultivated would pave the way for a secure and prosperous future. Mathematics was my comfort zone, familiar and logical, a stark contrast to the unpredictable emotional currents I struggled with at home. But with every theorem I solved and every economic model I studied, I found myself wanting to apply these academic pursuits to practical settings. I envisioned my career unfolding in the halls of banking or perhaps in the offices of a financial consultancy, oblivious to the fact that I was gradually distancing myself from my innate tendency to engage with the world on a human level.

However, as I approached the end of my undergraduate studies, I began to realise that my love for numbers could lead me in a different direction—one that combined my technical skills with my growing interest in tackling real-world challenges. Throughout my life, I have always sought practical applications for my knowledge, and I found myself drawn to the field of sales and solution selling. I understood that the analytical mindset I had developed through my economics degree would be a valuable asset in helping businesses identify their needs and implement effective solutions.

THE MOVE TO KUALA LUMPUR: A NEW BEGINNING

After completing my Bachelor's degree in Economics, I made a bold decision. I moved from Penang to Kuala Lumpur, Malaysia's bustling capital, to pursue a career in sales. The transition was significant for me, both personally and professionally. The fast-paced, high-energy environment of

Kuala Lumpur was a far cry from the quieter life I had known in Penang. Yet, I was determined to seize the opportunities that the big city had to offer.

I joined a technology company in Kuala Lumpur, beginning my career in Sales and Solution Selling. Although my background in economics wasn't directly related to sales, I quickly realised that the analytical skills I had honed during my studies were invaluable in understanding customer needs and identifying tailored solutions. My ability to break down complex problems, combined with my strong communication skills, allowed me to thrive in a customer-facing role.

In my primary role, I engaged with businesses to understand their pain points and present technology solutions that could help them achieve their goals. I found immense satisfaction in solving problems and guiding companies through the often complex world of technology and business transformation. Rather than just selling a product, my focus was on providing value by offering customised solutions that addressed each client's unique challenges.

My understanding of both the technical aspects of the solutions and my clients' business needs made me an exceptional sales professional. I was able to bridge the gap between the technical teams and the clients, ensuring the solutions we provided not only met their immediate needs but also aligned with their long-term business objectives. My economics background gave me an edge, as I could speak to the financial implications of different solutions, helping clients see the return on investment and long-term value.

THE GRIEF OF LOSS: NAVIGATING PERSONAL CHALLENGES

As my career flourished, life threw more challenges my way. The COVID-19 pandemic, which swept across the world, brought with it not only professional uncertainty but also personal loss. My beloved grandmother, the woman who had been my rock, passed away after battling health complications exacerbated by the pandemic. Losing her was a crushing blow, and I found myself struggling to cope with the void her death left in my life.

Yet, just as I was beginning to find some semblance of peace, tragedy struck again. My mother, who had always been my greatest supporter, succumbed to a sudden illness. The grief was overwhelming, and my heart broke once more. The weight of losing her felt unbearable, a gaping hole in my life that no amount of work or success could fill. It wasn't long before I also lost my father, who had been a steady presence throughout my life. His passing was a profound shock, and it compounded the already heavy sorrow of my recent losses.

Despite my grief, I continued to work hard, pouring myself into my professional life. My grandmother's teachings about resilience and perseverance became a source of strength during this difficult time. I had always found comfort in my work, and I used my success in my career as a way to honour her memory. However, the emotional toll of the pandemic, along with the loss of other family members, was something I couldn't easily escape.

As I navigated this period of grief, I began to realise that my career success wasn't just about hitting targets or closing deals—it was about the relationships I built, the trust I earned, and the value I provided to my clients. I found a deeper sense of purpose in my work, knowing that I could make a positive impact, even amid global uncertainty.

SUCCESS IN SALES AND SOLUTION SELLING

Today, I am a respected professional in the field of sales and solution selling, known for my ability to solve complex problems and deliver tailored solutions to clients. My success is not just a result of my technical knowledge and analytical skills; it also stems from my ability to connect with people, understand their needs, and provide value through meaningful, long-term solutions. My approach is built on trust, collaboration, and a deep understanding of my clients' challenges. In an industry where quick wins are often prioritised, I have stayed true to my philosophy of building lasting relationships and offering real value.

Despite the professional success I have achieved, my journey has not been without hardship. The loss of my grandmother and other relatives during the pandemic has profoundly shaped my outlook on life, reinforcing the importance of resilience and family. As I look toward the future, I remain passionate about my work. I continuously strive to build meaningful connections with clients and colleagues alike. I am also focused on giving back, mentoring others in my industry, and using my experiences to help others navigate the challenges of career and personal growth.

VALUABLE LIFE LESSONS LEARNT

First, resilience is crucial when faced with personal upheavals. Adversities, such as family disruptions, can be challenging, but finding a steady source of support—like my grandmother's silent strength—can help one navigate emotional complexities. This teaches us that perseverance and hope can transform even the most difficult situations into opportunities for growth.

Second, education and skill development provide a foundation for future success. Immersing myself in mathematics and economics not only honed my analytical skills but also provided a structured way to understand and engage with the world. It reminds me that investing in one's education equips us with tools that can open doors to various opportunities and empower us to adapt to changing circumstances.

Furthermore, adaptability is essential for personal and professional growth. Embracing change, such as my move from Penang to Kuala Lumpur, shows the importance of stepping out of one's comfort zone to seize new opportunities. This adaptability becomes a catalyst for growth and self-discovery.

Another key lesson is the value of relationship-building and providing meaningful contributions. In my career, I learned that success is not just about technical proficiency but also about understanding stakeholders' needs and offering tailored solutions. This underscores the importance of creating trust and collaboration in any professional endeavour.

Finally, integrating analytical skills with empathy can lead to more fulfilling work and personal experiences. By balancing intellectual rigor with an understanding of human connections, one can make impactful contributions and navigate the complexities of life with confidence. My journey illustrates that combining these elements fosters not only professional success but also a deeper sense of personal fulfilment and contribution.

ABOUT THE AUTHOR

Millie Yong Boon Hwei is a seasoned professional in the IT industry, with over 25 years of experience. For the past 20 years, she has worked with both local and multinational corporations, assisting small and medium-sized businesses (SMBs) and financial services institutions (FSIs) on their digital transformation journeys and innovation goals.

As the Director of Solution Sales at Microsoft, Millie assists SMBs and FSIs in adopting cloud computing to enhance productivity and customer experiences. Previously at IBM, she led teams in developing resilient systems for financial organisations.

Millie is dedicated to diversity, inclusion, and community engagement, supporting initiatives for individuals with disabilities and underprivileged communities during the COVID-19 pandemic. She is also actively involved with organisations like Lead Women and Women in Tech Malaysia.

Recently, she received the Asia Women Leaders Award 2024 and the prestigious Global Woman Influence Award 2024, recognising her impactful leadership in the IT industry.

YOU CAN CONNECT WITH MILLIE AT:

LinkedIn: *https://www.linkedin.com/in/millieyong/*
Email: *Millie.Yong@microsoft.com*

Story Eleven

NAVIGATING FINANCIAL INDEPENDENCE

Building Empowerment and Confidence Through Personal Experience and Resilience.

Some of my earliest memories revolve around watching my mother head off to work while I attended preschool and kindergarten. She was always home by the time I returned, but I never understood how unusual that was compared to other households where mothers stayed at home during the day. By the age of 10, I was a latchkey child, letting myself into the house after school and waiting for Mum to arrive around 4:30 PM. This responsibility made me fiercely independent and confident—traits that have remained with me into adulthood.

Throughout my life, my mother served as a significant role model. A New Zealander, she earned a degree in accounting in the 1950s, travelled the world as a single woman, and relocated to a new country after marrying. Even after we were old enough for school, she continued her career. She instilled in my sister and me the importance of independence, responsibility, and pursuing our dreams.

Reflecting on her impact, I realise she led by example—a true trailblazer—demonstrating how to embrace life and showing us that with determination, we could achieve a wide array of goals.

In my early 20s, I envisioned a future in the suburbs, focusing on my career and eventually marrying and starting a family. I anticipated tying the knot around the age of 30, after establishing myself as an accountant. The cosy, safe city of Sydney felt like my forever home, and I had no desire to leave. Yet, how mistaken I was to think that the next chapter of my life would unfold in the complete opposite manner!

In the early 1990s, while I was in my early 20s, I met my husband at work. He was a computer operator assigned to fix the computers in our office. Relatively new to Sydney and without a social circle, he often accompanied my friends and me on our outings every Friday and Saturday night. What began as friendship blossomed into romance after a few months. I quickly noticed his deep fascination with aircraft; he would always look up to identify every plane flying overhead. With a little encouragement, he decided to pursue his passion for flying, setting in motion a journey that continues over 30 years later.

Our marriage, however, was unconventional from the start. In our first two years, we spent only six months together, as he chased his dream of becoming a pilot. I understood how important this was to him and was committed to supporting him in any way I could. His path took him to Darwin, Vietnam, and Hong Kong, where he worked for minimal or no pay, amassing the flight hours needed to achieve his long-term goal of joining a major airline. During this time, I remained focused on my career in Sydney. Although it was challenging, we managed to stay connected through phone calls, as there were no digital platforms like Zoom or WhatsApp back then. Looking back, I realise that all our sacrifices have been worthwhile.

Despite the struggles, I continued working in Sydney, as most of his jobs offered little financial reward. Even with my modest income, I made sure to send him small amounts of money for his expenses. Our budget was incredibly tight—I allocated myself just $50 a week, half of which went to petrol for my car to commute to work. I believed that these sacrifices were essential for our future; by managing our finances wisely now, we were opening the door to limitless possibilities down the road. This dedication allowed my husband to pursue his dreams, reinforcing that following our individual passions was equally important.

A crucial aspect of our marriage has always been recognising one another as equal partners. My husband encourages me to chase my passions, just as I support him in his endeavours.

With a desire for independence, a sense of exploration, and the pursuit of new experiences, we made the bold decision to move to Hong Kong. Having only travelled to Australia, New Zealand, and Fiji, relocating to Hong Kong felt like a giant leap into the unknown. This was a time before the internet, when travel blogs detailing adventures and misadventures were not readily available, so I hopped on a plane with little knowledge of what awaited me.

I still vividly remember the day I arrived at the bustling Kai Tak Airport, burdened with about 100 kg of luggage. As I stood at the top of the ramp, I craned my neck, trying to spot my husband among the throngs of people in the arrival hall. This was my welcome to Hong Kong, and my mind raced with a flurry of thoughts—what was I doing here?

Being an expat, especially as a pilot's wife, comes with its own set of ups and downs. While it might sound glamorous, with Instagram posts showcasing travel, exotic dining, and poolside lounging, the reality is often more complex. Idleness is not something I handle well. Raised to be independent—with a working mother as my role model and a high school culture that emphasised higher education and career aspirations—I never imagined that I would find myself without work or the ability to contribute to our partnership.

After settling into our new country, I immediately began my job search. Unfortunately, I faced numerous rejections due to my lack of local language skills and experience. Eventually, I secured a position that I truly enjoyed, and I was fortunate enough to have a helper, allowing me to balance my career while also raising my children. Knowing I could continue my career provided me with a sense of financial security. I always felt reassured that if anything were to happen to my partner or if we needed to separate, I could support us. We had a plan: should he lose his job, we could return to Australia, where I could provide for us while he stocked supermarket shelves, and we would be okay.

To me, this financial independence is crucial in a relationship. I was fortunate to find a husband who embraced the idea of being equal partners, both financially and emotionally. Our earnings were pooled together, reflecting our collective effort towards financial stability. We have worked hard together to achieve our current level of financial security, something that would likely have been challenging to accomplish alone. My upbringing—marked by independence and curiosity—has been instrumental in helping me adapt to a new life in a place where I knew no one and was unfamiliar with the culture or language.

What helped me navigate this transition were several key aspects:

1. **Engage in clubs, sports, or activities that interest you**: This is where you'll connect with like-minded individuals who share similar passions while coming from diverse backgrounds. After arriving in Hong Kong, I joined a netball team and, over the years, have also coached rugby, played, umpired netball, and actively participated in both club and national associations for these sports.
2. **Stay persistent in your job search**: Don't be disheartened by setbacks. I faced numerous rejections, often being told that my lack of local language skills and experience were barriers. However, I remained undeterred. I networked and persevered, and eventually, my determination paid off. My first job in Hong Kong was with a major international bank, which I secured by directly sending my CV to the CFO. He called me to say he thought I was a good fit for a role and invited me for an interview. I obtained the position and stayed for over a decade. My commitment to advancing my career never wavered.
3. **Cultivate the ability to make decisions independently**: In a marriage, the expectation is to make significant life decisions together. However, as a pilot's wife, this wasn't always possible. For instance, when my son suddenly developed appendicitis, my husband was flying over the Middle East, and we had no means of communication. I had to make the urgent decision to take him to the hospital and proceed with the surgery without being able to consult his father. This experience reinforced my confidence

in my decision-making skills, and it's an empowering realisation that I cherish.

All of these strategies helped me settle into life in Hong Kong and adapt to my new surroundings. Throughout my time here, I've observed many relationships struggle, but I believe that being flexible, open to change, and embracing the wonders of a new country and culture contribute greatly to finding happiness as an expat.

Over the past decade, I have witnessed the dissolution of many long-term relationships and marriages among my friends. This experience has led me to understand the crucial importance of being aware of one's personal financial position. Many of my friends never learned to grasp their finances; they assumed that their marriages would endure until death do them part and that they would enjoy a comfortable retirement together. As an accountant, I often found myself assisting them in understanding their financial standing as they navigated the divorce process. My training allows me to explain financial positions and future needs clearly, but I quickly realised that compassion was equally essential. These individuals needed reassurance that they were not alone, and I wanted to offer the kind of support I would want if I were in their shoes.

Through my work, I've come to appreciate the significance of budgeting and profitability when it comes to running a business. Shareholders expect returns, and if those returns are lacking, it's crucial to determine what changes can be made to improve future performance. So, why don't we apply the same approach to our personal finances? If I were managing my own company, I would ensure that the financial records were up to date each month, assessing whether the business was profitable or running at a loss, and checking that there was enough cash flow.

However, not many people manage their personal finances with the same rigour they apply to their business. I, too, have been guilty of this oversight. My husband and I have faced both good times and challenges regarding our savings and spending. There have been moments when we overspent, accumulated credit card debt, and subsequently had to tighten our belts to reach our financial goals. Much of this learning has been self-taught. We often feel embarrassed when we have to cut back on outings to save money after overspending the previous month.

But I question: why should we feel this way? We are all human, and we all make mistakes. Many people find themselves in similar situations, and sometimes it takes swallowing our pride and seeking help to overcome these challenges.

My passion over the past five years has been to empower individuals to understand their finances, enabling them to make informed decisions. It's important to realise that managing your finances is not as complicated as it may seem. Whether or not you're comfortable with numbers, the concept is straightforward: money comes in, and money goes out.

I encourage everyone reading this to take a close look at their financial situation—be it their job, a personal business they've created, or their personal finances. Approach your personal finances with the same enthusiasm and attention to detail you would apply to evaluating your professional performance, whether it involves meeting sales targets or staying under budget for monthly expenses.

By applying similar principles and diligence, you may be surprised by how you can improve your personal wealth and make informed decisions moving forward. Additionally, consider setting clear financial goals and regularly tracking your progress. Create a simple budget that works for you, and don't hesitate to reach out for guidance or resources, whether from a financial advisor or trusted friends. The journey towards financial literacy and confidence starts with small, consistent steps. Remember, the key is to stay proactive and engaged if you want to achieve financial independence.

ABOUT THE AUTHOR

Sherryn Hancock is an Australian accountant, CPA (Aust), with almost 30 years of experience specialising in budgeting and management accounting. Known for her ability to "look at the whole picture," she works with people to help them understand their relationship with money and how it has affected them in the past. Sherryn strives to give them the tools and confidence to be financially aware for life.

Sherryn is making a difference by championing women to have a voice and be confident when dealing with financial matters, which expands into all other facets of their lives. She has recently completed her psychology degree and is now on the Board of WEN Hong Kong (Women's Entrepreneur Network) as well as the Committee for the Hong Kong Collaborative Practices Group. She is a past president of Hong Kong Netball, a Junior Rugby coach, and has been a passionate netball player and umpire since the age of 10.

She is a co-author of the Amazon No.1 bestseller book, #My Voice - Vol. 4, and she recently received the Global Women of Influence Awards 2024.

YOU CAN CONNECT WITH SHERRYN AT:

LinkedIn: *https://www.linkedin.com/in/sherrynhancock/*
Facebook: *https://www.facebook.com/profile.php?id=100064001795148*
Website: *https://www.sherrynhancockcpa.com/*

Story Twelve

REJECTING REJECTION

Transforming Rejection into Opportunity.

BEING ORDINARY

If you were to see me on the street, you probably wouldn't bat an eye. I am an ordinary office worker, living an ordinary life, working an ordinary schedule. Perhaps that is why my unordinary dream of becoming a social media influencer was almost always met with the same response: "You think you can do what even I couldn't? That's impossible." I couldn't help but wonder—why are people so quick to discourage? Are real success stories only destined for films and books?

Fuelled by these questions, I threw myself into social networking platforms, creating content and seeking out people beyond my immediate circle who had defied the odds—people who thought like I did. I was determined to be far beyond ordinary.

MUNDANE? REALLY?

I spent nine intense years in my current role as a startup incubator. Every project, every initiative—I poured my heart and soul into each one. But eventually, I reached a point we all face at some stage: questioning my path. Am I moving forward or just stumbling in the dark? Seeking clarity, I reached out to a few people, hoping for honest feedback on the value of my work.

One of these people was a private equity professional from New York. As he reviewed my CV, he paused, raised an eyebrow, and said, "Your CV looks so mundane; anyone could do this. Isn't there anything special about it?"

His comment felt like a slap in the face. Mundane? After years of hard work, late nights, and pouring every ounce of myself into my role, all he saw was "mundane"? My heart pounded, but I kept my cool.

"Ah... well... let's see..." I began. "I once created a YouTube interview series featuring biotech experts from Korea and beyond. When it went live, it quickly drew thousands of views, catching the attention of the algorithm. A journalist even reached out for an interview, and eventually, it was picked up in an article."

This time, he raised his eyebrow, but it wasn't out of disdain. "That's interesting. Why isn't that in your CV?"

In that moment, I realised that my ability to create engagement was something truly special. Now, it was time to use it for myself.

A NAME IN THE INBOX

I was pouring everything I had into finding investors for the startups I incubate. After endless cold calls and relentless efforts from every angle, I finally managed to send an email to a partner at a well-known venture capital firm. When his reply finally came, it read: "This should be sent to the main inquiry address."

Receiving this message felt like a sucker punch. And then, a harsher reality settled in—if it was this hard for me, how much harder must it be for the startups I work with to simply get a meeting, to prove their worth, to make someone believe in their vision?

That moment was a wake-up call—a stark reminder that effort and sincerity alone don't always make a difference. I needed to do something to stand out from the other "ordinary" people out there. That's why I turned to social media, posting insights on investment and tech trends. Slowly, my posts began drawing attention from both startups and investors, and step by step, I started carving out a name for myself.

WHO WOULD READ THIS?

As a film enthusiast who's watched some films ten times over, I channelled that passion into crafting posts inspired by captivating startup biopics. To my surprise, my posts began to gain traction. What started with just a few views soon grew into hundreds, then thousands.

"Love what you're sharing!"

"I totally relate!"

Encouraging comments and likes poured in, sparking a hope that maybe, just maybe, I was starting to build a name for myself.

Then, one day, I met with a marketing representative from a business media outlet who had come to pitch a PR service for startups. After wrapping up the business side of things, we lingered over coffee, chatting casually. Feeling a surge of confidence from the countless comments and likes I had garnered, I decided to show him a few of my posts. His reaction shifted almost instantly—from interest to mockery.

"It's neither complex nor unique. Honestly, who's going to bother reading this?"

My cheeks burned with embarrassment. But this time, I didn't crumble. His words stung, yes, but they couldn't erase the truth: people were reading, following, and encouraging me to keep going. And that was enough.

A FANTASY, REALLY?

By the time I reached 10,000 followers on LinkedIn, I knew it was time to take the next step. I wanted to write a book—a chronicle of my journey in building a personal brand through social media networking.

As an avid reader of business and economics books, I can often be seen flipping through pages or posting reviews of the latest releases on social media. One day, I received a call from a publisher who wanted to send me a new book, hoping I would post a review after I had finished reading it. At first, he was warm and enthusiastic when we engaged in small talk. But when I casually mentioned my own idea of publishing a book, his attitude abruptly became cold.

"You're no celebrity. The idea that you could publish a book and sell even a thousand copies is pure fantasy."

Once again, I found myself at a crossroads. But instead of letting the rejection stop me in my tracks, I chose a different path: I would self-publish. If no one else believed in my story, then I would. Armed with nothing but a dream and the guidance of online courses, I plunged headfirst into the world of self-publishing.

My sister, a talented writer, became an essential part of my project, helping with the editing. For the English version,

I collaborated with Jeremy On, a college consultant from Emory University, who took on the translation and editing. Every evening after work, I burned the midnight oil; I was determined to make my book a reality. By December—four months after I decided to put my ideas on paper—the Korean version of my book was finally ready.

I'll never forget the day I announced the release: the responses I received were overwhelming. My social media feed lit up with congratulations, photos of people proudly holding copies, and heartfelt messages from readers. They had followed my journey, and seeing me take on the challenge of publishing and succeed inspired them as well.

Then, just when I thought it couldn't get any better, I received the news on Christmas Day: A prominent tech media outlet in Singapore had named me one of their Top 10 Female Contributors. My followers were all cheering, and it felt almost unreal—as if I were living a dream.

THE CALL I DIDN'T EXPECT

One day, I received a phone call that stopped me dead in my tracks. On the other end was a reporter from one of Korea's major newspapers.

"I'm preparing an article about LinkedIn's growth in South Korea," she began. "Would you be available for an interview?"

Stunned, I managed to ask, "How did you hear about me?"

Her response left me speechless.

"I reached out to the media team at LinkedIn's U.S. headquarters and asked them to recommend a Korean LinkedIn influencer. They gave me one name: yours."

It felt surreal, almost impossible to believe. My name had reached LinkedIn's headquarters in the U.S. I'll never forget the moment I saw my name mentioned in an article that showcased me as a LinkedIn influencer, highlighting the tips I'd shared to help others build their digital presence using AI tools.

IT'S ABOUT IMPACT, NOT NUMBERS

One day, I opened my inbox to find an email with a subject line that made my heart skip a beat:

"Congratulations!!! You are the Winner of The Global Women of Influence Awards 2024."

For the first time in my life, I found myself travelling to Singapore to attend an international awards ceremony. As I stepped onto the stage, surrounded by powerful, accomplished women from around the world, my heart pounded. Taking a steadying breath, I looked out at the audience and began: "When I first started posting on social media, my audience was pretty much just a few friends and my sister. Today, my posts reach over a million views. But I've learned that it's not the number of followers or connections that truly matters—it's the impact of the message you put out there. Let's continue to inspire and be the positive change we want to see for women everywhere."

The applause that followed wasn't merely a sound in the room—it felt like a wave, echoing across social media. My followers, those who had been with me since the very beginning, were there virtually, cheering me on. In that moment, I realised just how far I'd come.

THE BOOK ON THE SHELF

After publishing my book, I often faced the same question from people: "How many copies have you sold?" Their curiosity focused on the numbers, as if the success of my book could only be measured by sales figures.

But the responses from seasoned professionals—leaders in various fields, some even bestselling authors—felt different. They were more interested in the journey itself: "Publishing a book is impressive!" or, "What inspired you to publish it in English?" They seemed to recognise the courage it takes to put something into the world.

As the publisher had anticipated, my book wasn't a bestseller. Yet, it found a place in over 30 libraries, including the "Marketing" section of the National Sejong Library, where it sits beside the works of well-known authors.

I shared this news with my followers, and as I scrolled through the responses, one reaction stood out. A prominent macroeconomics expert—someone I'd only ever seen on TV or in books—had 'liked' my post. I sent a quick note thanking him, and his reply was warm: "Congratulations once again! Keep pushing forward, and I wish you continued success!"

I was no longer just Dongmi; I was Homo Dongmicus. And I was far beyond ordinary.

HOMO DONGMICUS: FAR BEYOND ORDINARY

When I first set out, my goal was clear: to become a trusted figure in the startup world, someone investors could rely on to help promising startups secure the funding they needed. But as my journey unfolded, I began to notice that people viewed me as more than just a writer or startup expert. They saw "Dongmicus, the Icon of Challenge and Action."

Yes, the challenges were daunting—I faced more "no's" than I could count. However, I am now recognised as an expert in digital personal branding and storytelling, and I've found doors opening that I never imagined: invitations to speak at seminars, appearances on regional radio, a TV lecture, and even guest spots on YouTube.

Eventually, I realised that what set me apart was my willingness to be genuine, to show the world exactly who I am. This authenticity became my strength, allowing me to carve out a name in a fiercely competitive space.

Recently, I joined a global mentorship program and met my mentee, Richard Tran—a multiple-term elected mayor in California who transitioned to become a startup founder, launching HR solutions for the manufacturing industry in Vietnam. During his visit to Korea, he left me with words that reignited my ambition:

"This is just your first book. Keep sharing your voice in new ways—through different formats and beyond."

So, should I take the next step? Absolutely. I'm Homo Dongmicus, and I'm ready to go even further. I am not ordinary—I am far beyond it.

Embracing authenticity and resilience can transform challenges into opportunities for growth and recognition. By being true to oneself and remaining committed to a vision, it's possible to evolve beyond ordinary expectations. Therefore, I would say always be open to evolving your approach and exploring new ways to share your voice and expertise..

ABOUT THE AUTHOR

Sarah Dongmi Choi is a Senior Manager at the Chungbuk Center for Creative Economy and Innovation, a non-profit backed by South Korea's Ministry of SMEs and Startups. As a leader in digital branding, she empowers individuals to enhance their careers and businesses through a robust global digital presence. Her LinkedIn posts, garnering over a million views annually, offer valuable insights into personal branding, technology, and investment trends.

As the author of Homo Dongmicus: The Evolution from an Office Worker to an Influencer, Sarah shares her personal journey while offering actionable tips on personal branding and opinion leadership. Recognised as one of e27's "Top 10 Women Contributors Spearheading Resilience in the Startup Landscape," she continues to inspire entrepreneurs and investors alike with her innovative approach and commitment to fostering growth within the startup community. Sarah also won the prestigious Global Women of Influence Award 2024 for her contribution to society.

YOU CAN CONNECT WITH SARAH DONGMI AT:

LinkedIn: *www.linkedin.com/in/dongmicus/*
Facebook: *www.facebook.com/dongmicus*
Website: *www.dongmicus.com*

Story Thirteen

RISING ABOVE EXPECTATIONS

Awareness, Communication & Empowerment.

Coming from a middle-class family, I believed that financial independence was the point, a final score of a fulfilled and secure life. I was proud to be the first female on my father's side of the family to build a stable and independent life. When I stepped into the most important relationship of life, I inherited the ***expectation*** of my partner being the main earner of the family. But I was proud and confident that with my growing career, we will be able to make our life better and enjoy all those things, which seemed difficult before.

It didn't take long for me to realise that independence was about more than financial stability. It's about emotional and psychological resilience, liberation from unreasonable standards either put on me by others or that I have imposed on myself, and the courage to make choices consistent with my values, even when they go against the grain of society.

I endured eight years with someone I knew within the first two years wouldn't last. Where I wanted to grow and build a secure future, he seemed content chasing short-term pleasure, a state of ***transient gratification***. And I recall bitterly the numerous occasions he'd spent big things he couldn't actually afford but been paying for from my savings, and the way he explained it away as "living life."

Our differences went beyond money; my expectations from life and my partner invaded every nook of our lives. He didn't cheer on my achievements. Instead, his vices grew, his spending increased, and I felt ***less like a partner and more like a provider***, someone whose achievements were an excuse to indulge. Over time, I started to see the subtle grinding down of joy in my life. Even the laughter that used to come easily felt forced. Work, once a place of passion and creativity, became an escape, an option to avoid the emptiness brooding at home.

I normally cheered family and friend's happiness, but it was always in my heart like an arrow. The absence of feeling noticed, appreciated, and cared for just grew deep. I remember countless occasions when I wore my smile when all that blossomed in my soul was a hollow heart, a pang in my chest, reminding me of the space that was filled in my life.

Another expectation that my family wanted me to continue this relationship at any cost was burdening and wrong. When I decided to take steps to quit, the unwavering support of my family was so liberating. It wasn't one major event that made me realise I had to get out. It had built gradually over the years, small things that kept accumulating. The more I felt unseen or taken for granted, the little bit of me that had gotten unearthed started to slip away. Inside, I knew I couldn't keep living in a place that dulled my shine.

Choosing myself didn't come as a snap decision. It was the product of a million little epiphanies all pointing the same way: "I needed to prioritise myself." I did not quit with blame or anger but an understanding that we both deserve someone who complimented us.

FREE FROM UNMET EXPECTATIONS

Breaking free from unfulfilling expectations wasn't a momentary big decision, it was a process of tiny, conscious steps toward becoming aware and owning the process of your life. To work on my life and fill the void that was created.

Socially, when I watched friends, colleagues, and family members build their lives around children after marrying, I told myself I wanted this as well. At one point, I craved a baby solely because it seemed like the "***normal***" thing to do as an adult, not out of some emotional bond or mutual directive toward the same future.

Eventually, I let myself face the bigger truth. I needed to reconstruct my identity, discover what truly mattered to me, and decide what would make me happy and content. This was when I began my deliberate journey toward designing a life aligned with my values and desires.

What I have today, my present relationship, is one of ***respect, joy, and growth***. Together, we celebrate life's moments, grow from its lessons, and support each other wholeheartedly. This is the kind of relationship that ***feeds the soul instead of draining it***, one where both of us can be better versions of ourselves. When my second relationship began, everything felt different. All the little things I ever hoped for in a partner started coming true. I remember ***smiling a lot***, enjoying every second, not wanting it to end.

I made a conscious effort to bring the lessons from my first relationship and life experiences into this one. What helped most were my ***coaching skills***, non-judgment, empathy, and active listening, which became my toolkit for nurturing and growing this partnership.

THE ACE TRANSFORMATION

At a later stage, the decision to become a Coach became my guiding light—without it, my evolution would not have been possible. Through coaching, I discovered what I have come to call my superpowers: **Awareness, Communication, and Empowerment (ACE)**

- **Awareness** taught me to observe and recognise my thoughts and emotions without judgment, enabling me to better differentiate between what society says I want and what I actually do.
- **Communication** enabled me to express my needs to others directly and compassionately, navigate conflicts, and build stronger bonds.
- **Empowerment** was releasing guilt, establishing boundaries, and realising the liberty found in being one's true self.

These superpowers laid the groundwork for my day-to-day life and all of the challenges I faced with clarity and perseverance.

LETTING GO

In my last relationship, I ended up taking on all the responsibilities, both financially and otherwise. It was no longer just a chore; it had turned into a rite, a tacit law I needed to adhere to. It was my form of caring and love. I did what was wanted and needed, ran the household, worked things around, literally everything, even if it wore my soul thin.

I had gotten so stuck in this provider and caretaker role that it had become mouldy and clinging, something I couldn't escape from. I built this armour around myself to protect myself from vulnerability and failure, but it also stopped me from accepting help from those who cared about me.

Gradually, I learned that my defensiveness was more than just a shield; it was the residue of deeper emotional wounds. This realisation took time to unpack, but it finally helped me understand the core of my resistance.

So when I stepped into my second relationship, the most difficult part was the vulnerability and also allowing someone to love me the way I loved and sharing roles in the relationship. I had to let go of the belief that I had to do everything on my own. Giving myself the vulnerability of receiving, of trusting that I could be working off someone else for a bit, was the breakthrough I'd been waiting for. The acceptance was a turning point in my healing journey as I learned that love doesn't mean having to bear the whole world on your shoulders alone.

When I let go of the unreasonable standards and expectations I placed on myself, the pressure of perfectionism started to lessen. I learned to be more reflective, more restrained in my reactions, and more willing to ask for help. This new perspective freed me, helping me grow in ways I never imagined and approach challenges with a calm I hadn't experienced in years.

By embracing acceptance, practicing vulnerability, and maintaining a renewed sense of empowerment, I learned to approach my relationships, both personally and professionally, with empathy and resilience.

THE F.I.R.E. FRAMEWORK: A TOOL FOR SELF-REFLECTION

Along the way, I created the F.I.R.E. Framework to help guide self-reflection and growth:

1. **Frequency**: How often do unmet expectations cause frustration? Are there recurring patterns?
2. **Intensity**: What is the impact of unmet expectations on your feelings and decisions?
3. **Reflection**: Do you have realistic expectations? Are you making your needs clear?
4. **Empowerment**: Which small steps are you able to take to bring your actions into alignment with your values?

This then cemented itself as a go to framework for me as I began to do the work of how expectations were impacting my well-being and focus. Though I had done this personal work, I immediately started spiralling again—being concerned with ***others' expectations***.

I came deeply to this realisation on my last birthday. I didn't expect ostentatious celebrations, but I did expect thoughtful wishes from family and friends who had always remembered in the past. This year, several of the most important people in my life either forgot to wish me or ***didn't do so in a way I silently wished*** they would.

It wasn't that I didn't receive birthday greetings or that people forgot; it was the ***weight of my own unmet expectations***, a burden I unknowingly made for myself. Add on the professional disappointments, like lost opportunities, leads that went cold, peers and clients who didn't follow through on commitments. Here was yet another weight of emotional expectations.

And I realised that it wasn't actually realistic ***to expect that same level of investment, perfection, and care*** — both in work and in life — out of others that I demand of myself. Not everyone is in the same place to give energy, love, compassion, and care. None of those expectations are bad in themselves, but their price in terms of the emotional cost of feeling unfulfilled, being disappointed or simply being ghosted by people became too high for me, a time to set boundaries around my expectations. I turned to self-awareness and empathy again as anchors to help me clarify again, and reconnect to my purpose.

For me, empowerment means not controlling others but rather creating a space where I can thrive regardless of my environment.

Conversations are ***key*** to transforming awareness into action. As we begin to recognise our own inner patterns and struggles, we absolutely must open up to those who are important to us about what we are experiencing.

Reflective conversations—whether with a partner, friend, mentor, or even ourselves—help us process emotions, set boundaries, and align our relationships with our newfound clarity. Through these dialogues, we cultivate understanding, deepen connections, and create space for growth, both individually and collectively.

MOVING FORWARD WITH PURPOSE

Life often challenges in unplanned ways. Every experience, whether it stems from unmet expectations, personal struggles, or relevant transitions, will pave the road to the person you will become.

Brené Brown's quote inspires this journey for me: "*Daring to set boundaries is about having the courage to love ourselves, even when we risk disappointing others.*"

Empowerment starts the instant we understand that taking care of ourselves is not selfish but necessary. Choosing yourself is not an act of abandoning others, but it is showing up without resentment and from an authentic place.

I envision a world where awareness, empathy, and empowerment guide our choices. A world where I am surrounded by people who are open enough to have challenging conversations and the openness to grow.

I will continue my journey by coaching myself and people through their own stories, helping them break free of the invisible chains and limiting beliefs that can bind them. I do this to inspire reflective conversations with myself and with the people who matter in my life.

"UNMET YET EMPOWERED"

Expectations rise, a silent tide,
Dreams of others walking beside.
Yet when they falter, fail, or fall,
I learn to stand despite it all.

Empathy whispers, a gentle guide,
Through disappointments, I confide.
Boundaries drawn with loving grace,
A newfound peace, I now embrace.

The journey inward, the truest art,
Where awareness dwells within the heart.
To thrive, to love, to persevere,
Empowered now, my path is clear.

With clarity and growth, I guide others near."

REFLECT AND EMPOWER YOURSELF

And as you look back on your own life, think about these questions:

- What expectations from your culture, family, or society have you internalised?
- How, in turn, do they influence your decisions today?
- What would it mean to choose yourself in your circumstances?

But no matter where you are, keep in mind:

- **Awareness** is the first step toward transformation.
- **Communication** strengthens relationships.
- **Empowerment** is the key to living authentically.

Embrace your own superpowers. Trust your journey. You are capable, deserving, and worthy of a life filled with peace and fulfilment.

ABOUT THE AUTHOR

Vedika Khatwani Chandka is an ACC-credentialed ICF Coach, Trainer, Mentor, and Facilitator and the founder of EmpowerUrself, a space where self-awareness meets empowerment. With nearly two decades of corporate experience, including roles as an Executive Assistant to C-suite leaders and an HR Business Partner, Vedika brings a deep understanding of personal and professional development.

Her own journey of overcoming limiting beliefs and cultivating confidence forms the foundation of her coaching. Specialising in self-awareness, emotional intelligence, IKIGAI and applied psychology, she offers a compassionate yet results-driven approach to help clients navigate challenges, build clarity, and take empowered action.

Based in the UAE, Vedika blends soft skills training and tailored coaching to help individuals transform aspirations into achievements. Known for her calm and insightful coaching style, she inspires her clients to embrace growth, align with their values, and thrive in every aspect of life. She loves to read and have reflective and impactful conversations.

YOU CAN CONNECT WITH VEDIKA AT:

LinkedIn: *https://www.linkedin.com/in/vempowerurself/*
Website: *https://vempowerurself.com/*
YouTube: *www.youtube.com/@vempowerurself*

Story Fourteen

RISING BEYOND

From Invisible to Divine.

MY STORY

I was not born with presence, and perhaps that is why I have been obsessed with it. I have felt invisible for most of my life. Now, my daughters inspire me to show up unabashedly and unapologetically. Raising great women means being a great role model. I would not do anything that I would not want my daughters to emulate. Here is my story of the ghosts of my past and the angels of the future who made me who I am today.

In truth, the only way to put ghosts to rest is to bring them out of the closet, acknowledge them, and let them go. Ghosts must be recognised as they are searching for a voice. Until they are heard and recognised, they seek to stay and become a presence in your life.

It is the revenge of the ghosts that remain unacknowledged that can get in the way of you becoming your best self, which will enable you to move your dreams forward to fruition in your life. Ultimately, it is important to acknowledge who you are independent of conditioning. It is like addressing the proverbial elephant in the room. Here are two such elephants I am setting free now—. Read about them, and I hope my little release sets you free, too.

By all accounts, my upbringing had all the potential to be idyllic and privileged. But by the age of four, my engineer father fell sick with meningitis. My four-year-old self couldn't understand what was happening. My mother would disappear for days, staying with my father at various hospitals. The family would tell me he was in a coma. Confused, quiet, and too lost for words to express myself, I remember thinking coma was the name of the hospital room. My brother and I were shunted from relative to relative. In some places, we were welcome, and in some places, we clearly weren't. I remember myself becoming quieter, introspective, and observant—just living in my own company. I also became intensely protective of my younger brother; in essence, I became his 5-year-old mother.

It was, to say the least, a confusing time. I knew I had to be more responsible, but there was no manual. A nagging feeling that I was to do something to help to make the situation better if not for my parents but for my brother. No one told me, and I didn't ask.

One of my earliest memories is of looking at the swimming pool that my father was constructing for me at the back of the house. The rectangular hole was dug in the backyard and while he was in the hospital, the monsoons had started. Dirty water began filling up my dear father's precious gift to me. Every day, when the rain stops briefly, I run to the back of the house to stare into the hole, and my heart breaks. I still remember those days clearly. I would look up at the sky and ask the Gods to stop the water, just for three days. I was sure my father would come home in a few days and put up the blue tiles and fill the pool with "blue water."

Many years later, I often wondered if it was still there, that ominous rectangular hole in the middle of our three-acre backyard. It was the focus of my daily prayers to the rain gods—a desperate plea of a little girl in eastern India in the late 1970s.

But my father never came home. He was taken to Calcutta on a plane as his condition worsened. This was the closest I had come to a plane in my young life and I stood, intimidated. The airport was just a room and an airstrip. My father lay unconscious on a stretcher on the ground, and my mother standing next to him. As they waited to board the flight, they told me again he was in a coma. I was choking up and trying to put up a brave face, and I knew I didn't want to know what a coma was anymore. I saw them put him on the plane, and my mother joined him. Soon, the plane was a small speck in the sky, and then it disappeared. I stood there immobile until someone carried me back to the car, feeling abandoned and confused. After the flight took them away to Calcutta, we were never a family again.

Nevertheless, my life would have regained a level of normalcy within a few years, even without my father. However, what followed were turbulent years as we moved several times. Perhaps, in part, due to the unsettled nature of our lives, I experienced sexual and physical abuse at the hands of an acquaintance. Luckily, this eventually stopped once we were able to move away from the offender.

But these early experiences form us and have a great impact on our lives, as they certainly had on mine as I now parent two young girls.

NOT SO LONG AGO

I received a call from my friend, a Swiss art advisor who is involved with an international art installation featuring men and women who have faced sexual assault. She wanted me to be one of twenty-five survivors of sexual assault who would be featured. The installation will be displayed in London and perhaps travel to other parts of the world.

After the call, feeling unsettled, I sat by myself and considered whether I really wanted to share this story publicly. What would this accomplish? Then my next thought was, what if my then-9-year-old daughter were to find out about it? If I did share my story publicly, how would this impact her? It was my job to protect her from the ugliness of the world, perhaps because I could see my young self easily reflected in her eyes.

I sat down with her to share a version of the story that she could make sense of and understand. She is already very aware of what sexual inappropriateness is. My experiences have made me perhaps an overly cautious mother, and I would rather she know that any violation of her personal space is not ever acceptable or okay. I told her that if I did share my story in the international art installation, I wanted to make sure that she would be okay with it.

My daughter said to me, "Ma, I know this has been difficult, and you are hurting, but it was not your fault. You don't need to hide. Please go ahead and do this. More people need to know that it is all right to talk about it. In fact, they should."

Tears began to roll down my face. I felt I had been set free. I felt an inexplicable pride at being her mother, yet I also felt like the tables had been turned, and I had momentarily become a child again, a child released of the burden I had been carrying around my whole life.

To look at the future, we need to set free the ghosts of the past. We must accept ourselves as we are at this moment... the sum total of all our potential, accomplished and unaccomplished.

THE PRESENT

Today, I have moved beyond my past conditionings. Although old ghosts may occasionally surface, I now remind myself that I am worthy of love and reverence. This realisation emerged after hitting rock bottom when I reflected on my children and vowed not to pass on my trauma. The intention that "it ends with me" became a powerful motivator.

Healing can be a painful journey. It requires confronting pain and letting go without anger or resentment, which can be even more challenging. My journey began with the affirmation: "I am divine." I realised that my worth is not defined by experiences, accomplishments, or possessions but by who I inherently am. My ancient culture teaches *Aham Brahmasmi*—"I am Brahman" or "I am the Divine." This reminds me that when I silence the external noise, the same force that drives the universe also propels me forward.

I refuse to be bound by society's expectations and judgments that come with the messages of "*shoulda*," "*coulda*," or "*oughta*." Recognising my true self is empowering. I am more than my traumas or the limitations imposed by societal norms; my essence remains untouched by what the world may consider imperfections. I am not here to conform to anyone else's definition of me. How you perceive me reflects your own self-view. Once I acknowledge my divinity, I also recognise the preciousness in others.

Born in the 1970s and navigating my teenage years in the 1990s, I experienced a world where women were often defined by societal expectations. You were expected to have a career while also being the perfect homemaker. While I fulfil my responsibilities, I strive for balance. Instead of chasing happiness, I seek equilibrium, which is a higher state of mind.

For over a decade, I have worked with a leadership and executive presence coach for women, developing transformative innate confidence. This confidence transcends accomplishments, reminding me that I am not better than anyone else; you and I are equal.

Humility is often misinterpreted as seeing oneself as inferior, but true humility recognises that everyone is equal and plays a vital role in the larger tapestry of life. This understanding came to me not through cosmic intervention but through the guidance of my spiritual mentor, who had a profound awareness of his own divinity. During one of my lowest moments, he came into my life and encouraged me to see my true self beyond past experiences., asking for nothing in return. His mentorship sparked a transformation within me. He taught me that true power is not given but recognised. Acknowledging this power diminished the angst I had clung to for so long.

As I learned to stop belittling myself, I shed guilt and

fear. Recognising my awareness provided me with newfound freedom, liberating me from the expectations of others—and even my own. Now, when old habits resurface, I know how to return to that freedom.

I have embraced regular spiritual practices, including meditation, visualisation, and acts of service. These practices help me block out external noise and connect with my true self, free from the "not enough" narrative I once believed. More often than not, I remind myself that I am a divine being navigating life, which empowers me to face challenges with resilience.

Serving others has become a cornerstone of my journey. My subconscious recognises my efforts to do good, fostering deep self-respect. I don't need to be grateful or acknowledged in return; simply helping others bolsters my sense of self-worth.

I realise it's about genuinely liking and respecting the person I see in the mirror. This self-respect diminishes the guilt and inadequacy that once plagued me. Embracing my divine nature allows me to watch my life unfold like a character in a movie—fully engaged yet aware it's just a role.

After years of feeling small and uncertain, I've learned that my worth isn't tied to perfection; it simply is. By sharing my experiences, I didn't erase myself; I liberated myself. Imagine a world where we all perceive ourselves as divine and worthy of respect. Would voices of doubt or shame still hold power?

Today, I invite you to see yourself as I see myself—divine and whole. Release your regrets, acknowledge your strengths, and embrace your sacredness. Remember, you are not separate from the divine; you are the divine. Embrace this truth, and shine in your fullness.

Aham Brahmasmi. Tat Tvam Asi.

You are that.

ABOUT THE AUTHOR

Devika M. Das is a seasoned Global Leadership Coach with a distinguished credential from INSEAD. She is dedicated to empowering leaders through transformational coaching. At CORE Executive Presence, she specialises in enhancing the leadership presence and effectiveness of C-suite executives and emerging leaders. She utilises her expertise to foster inclusivity and skill development.

As an active member of prestigious councils, including the Forbes Coaches Council and the Harvard Business Review Advisory Council, Devika excels at integrating psychodynamics with practical leadership strategies. Her commitment to diversity and inclusion is evident in her work, where she guides senior executives to strengthen their influence while cultivating more inclusive organisational cultures. Through her coaching, Devika helps leaders recognise and harness their unique strengths, fostering environments where all voices are valued and empowered.

Devika is a devoted mother to two wonderful teenage daughters, an artist with a passion for writing, and someone who engages in profound spiritual practices.

YOU CAN CONNECT WITH DEVIKA AT:

LinkedIn: *https://www.linkedin.com/in/dasdevika/*
Website: *https://www.devikadas.com/*
Instagram: *https://www.instagram.com/devikadascoaching/*

Story Fifteen

SHAPING MY NARRATIVE

From Struggles to Triumphs.

I'm 20 years old and in training to become a hairstylist, living one of my dreams. The journey to this moment has been shaped by a variety of experiences—uplifting lessons and challenging setbacks alike. Each moment has played an important role in shaping who I am today. Born and bred in the vibrant city of Hong Kong, I have experienced tremendous joy. However, my path has not been free of challenges. Among the most significant struggles I've faced is discrimination.

Coming to terms with the hurtful words directed at me and my family has been a big challenge, particularly when others assumed we didn't recognise their disapproval. While I have always tried to brush aside these incidents, they eventually took a toll on me. It feels disheartening to be treated differently in a place I proudly call home. Unlike many others around me, I speak Cantonese fluently, which has been an asset in building connections. It often surprises locals to hear me converse effortlessly in their language, and yet it makes me wonder why this is viewed as surprising in our interconnected world. In a time when multilingualism should be celebrated, it sometimes feels like an exception if the language spoken isn't English.

Discrimination has presented itself in various forms. I recall a particularly vivid incident from a few years ago when I suffered an accident that left my foot fractured. During my recovery, I had to rely on crutches for mobility, making even simple tasks feel impossible. Climbing stairs became a daily struggle, and despite my family's unwavering support, navigating this new reality was both painful and exhausting. What hurt even more was the discovery—after I had healed—that there had been a pathway designated for disabled individuals all along the route I frequently took, a path we were never alerted to. This experience highlights a painful truth about discrimination: It can show up in ways that many people do not notice, leaving those who need help to take care of themselves without the support they need.

Another recurring challenge I encountered was the discomfort and avoidance from strangers while using public transport. Often, people would refuse to sit next to me or would vacate their seats as soon as I settled into one. Much of this discrimination stemmed from how I looked, particularly as a Muslim woman donning modest clothing, including the hijab. Instead of fostering understanding, my appearance often aggravated the discrimination I faced, pushing some individuals further away.

To many, these actions may seem small, but for someone who faced them repeatedly during childhood, they leave a lasting mark. As a young person who struggled with confidence, these moments made me very sad and angry. Even though I considered this city my home, I often felt like an outsider. However, I want to highlight that despite these challenges, I have found my strength. I've learned ways to rise above my experiences and not let them control me.

One of the main influences that helped shape my journey was an amazing organisation called **Be The Change**. This charity became a lifeline for me during my childhood, guiding me in many areas of life, especially in education.

More importantly, it played a vital role in helping me build my self-confidence.

As children, we often find ourselves in a world full of uncertainties. We navigate the challenges of growing up, with each day bringing new tests to our strength and resilience. Whether it's facing a room full of classmates, speaking up in class, or simply sharing our thoughts and feelings, self-doubt can feel overwhelming. I remember my own childhood, filled with moments of hesitation and fear. I would often miss out on opportunities because my insecurities held me back. I was a wallflower at social events, afraid of judgment and failure.

Through these difficulties, I learned important lessons that shaped who I am today. Overcoming these struggles isn't just about building confidence; it's about embracing our unique qualities and recognising our worth. Each of us has a voice that deserves to be heard and a story that needs to be told. The key is to nurture that voice, even when it feels delicate.

It's important to remember that confidence is not a final goal; it's a journey. It starts with small steps like taking risks, facing our fears, and celebrating our achievements, no matter how tiny they seem. Being around supportive friends and mentors who lift us up can make a huge difference. Their encouragement helps us take brave steps forward, just like Be The Change did for me.

As we get older, we also need to learn how to quiet that inner critic—the voice that tells us we're not good enough. Instead, let's focus on self-love and acceptance. By recognising our struggles and embracing our imperfections, we can turn our weaknesses into strengths.

Speaking of strengths, let me explain more about how Be The Change became the guiding light I needed.

It's often said that a teacher is the second most important person in a child's life after their mother, and I completely agree. I am thankful that when I was just six or seven years old, my family found Be The Change, a place that helped us in many ways, especially with education. I feel lucky to have had this opportunity during such important years of my life. Because of Be The Change, I did well in school, but what I remember most is how much my self-confidence grew. I can't stress enough how important it is to have good role models and great mentors. Having supportive people around you can really change how you see your future.

It's perfectly okay to seek help for your future; in fact, it's something we should encourage. You may think, "I'm so young; I haven't achieved much compared to others." But I want to assure you that the experiences I've gained so far are immensely valuable to me. There are many individuals out there, just like me, who need someone to raise their voice and encourage them to follow their dreams.

Growing up, many of us were taught to believe in society's common ideas about career choices. We often hear that we should aim to become doctors, engineers, or teachers. While these professions are admirable and essential, they can sometimes lead to confusion for those of us whose passions lie in different areas. I went through various phases of wanting to pursue careers like being a doctor, a nurse, or even a teacher—not because those were my true passions, but because they were the paths I saw others taking. Deep down, I always knew that my true passion was to be a hair and beauty stylist.

After finishing high school, I took some time to think about my future. I didn't want to be stuck in a career that wouldn't bring me happiness. So, I tried out different jobs, including tutoring and working in the food and beverage industry. I never felt my time was wasted. In fact, these experiences only fuelled my interest in pursuing my passion even more. Nearly two years later, I found what I was looking for. I am now training and working at a top-rated salon, and I couldn't be happier.

However, my journey hasn't been without its challenges. Like many young women from ethnic backgrounds, I faced hurtful comments from authority figures. One memory stands out to me: a teacher once told me, "Why are you still studying? You should just quit; you're going to get married and take care of your husband anyway. What's the point of wasting your time and money on your studies?" These words were spoken to me right before my DSE exams, which are crucial for determining my future. Imagine the pressure of preparing for those exams while hearing such hurtful things from a trusted teacher.

I respect homemakers because I know it is one of the hardest jobs in the world. But hearing limiting words like that from a teacher was painful. It felt as though she didn't believe in my potential. However, I refused to let those negative thoughts define who I was. Instead, I used those comments as motivation to achieve more. Today, that same teacher shares my story as an example to inspire her students. For me, that is evidence of perseverance.

What I want to highlight in my story is that despite the discrimination and negative assumptions from teachers or loved ones, let those experiences motivate you to shine. Show others what you can achieve—not out of anger or revenge, but to fulfil your own sense of accomplishment. Whether you choose to work or be a homemaker, never let harsh words affect your performance. Use those comments as challenges to help you grow. Remember that your only competition is yourself. Strive to be better than you were yesterday.

We should all remember that everyone has their own battles. Some people emerge victorious, while others may need a voice to help lift them up. I aspire to be that voice for those who can relate to my journey. My story may not seem monumental, but even the smallest experiences can make a significant impact. If just one person can find inspiration in my words, then I have succeeded.

Despite these challenges, I remain committed to my dreams and aspirations. Each hurdle has taught me resilience and deepened my understanding of empathy. My experiences have fuelled my desire not only to excel in my chosen profession but also to foster inclusivity and understanding within my community. As I advance through my training, I am reminded of the power of kindness, the importance of self-acceptance, and the necessity of standing firm in the face of adversity. Each step I take brings me closer to my dream, and I am determined to illuminate a path for others navigating similar struggles. Together, we can create a world where diversity is not only accepted but celebrated, and where every individual feels valued and understood.

Everyone's path is different, and finding support can significantly impact your success. It's crucial to pursue your true passions, even if they diverge from societal norms. Taking time to explore various opportunities can lead you to your calling, with each experience contributing to your growth. While negative comments from respected individuals can be discouraging, use these moments to fuel your motivation and prove your worth.

It's essential to prioritise personal growth over comparison with others. Focus on your unique journey and recognise that everyone faces challenges; embracing these struggles can lead to resilience and inner strength. If you've faced adversity, consider sharing your story to uplift and encourage others on their paths. Lastly, seek accomplishments that bring you genuine fulfilment rather than merely fulfilling expectations set by society. By embracing these principles, readers can be inspired to pursue their dreams, overcome obstacles, and create a supportive community where individuals uplift one another in their unique journeys.

A journey of a thousand miles begins with a single step." – Lao Tzu

ABOUT THE AUTHOR

Bibi Muskaan Haider, at just 20 years old, is training to be a hairstylist, pursuing a lifelong dream fuelled by her passion for enhancing beauty. From a young age, she has enjoyed making others happy, viewing hairstyling as an art form that can transform lives.

Muskaan's dedication extends beyond hairstyling; she has also completed her studies and gathered three years of valuable experience in tutoring children. Her love for teaching shines through as she aims to positively impact her students' lives. Whether in a classroom or salon, her goal is to uplift and empower those around her. What truly sets Muskaan apart is her commitment to service.

Involved with the charity organisation Be The Change as she grew up, she gained essential values and aspirations. Inspired by her experiences, Muskaan is determined to be a guiding light for others in need, using her skills and kindness to uplift their spirits.

YOU CAN CONNECT WITH MUSKAAN AT:

LinkedIn: *https://www.linkedin.com/in/muskaan-bibi-haider-097a87231/*

Email: *muskaanbb@gmail.com*

Story Sixteen

THE PRIVILEGE AND HONOUR OF BEING A PARENT

The Key to Unlocking Effective Communication with Children.

'Four fifths of children appear to be "dandelions", who can thrive in most environments. The remaining fifth are "orchids", who are more exquisite and unusual and have a higher potential than dandelions – but for this to be realised they require a particular environment and careful gardening.' - Thomas Boyce

In bustling Hong Kong two decades ago, a mother embarks on a passionate journey to support her son, who faces the challenges of ADHD in an environment that often feels overwhelming. With a spine of steel and a heart full of love, she navigates the complexities of parenting an anxious child, determined to secure the accommodations he needs to thrive.

As she confronts social misconceptions, limited resources, and a lack of a solid support system, she battles the daily struggles of advocating for her son's needs in a city that often overlooks the importance of mental health.

This narrative explores the depths of a parent's duty, surprisingly strong determination, and her life's mission to secure a happy future for her child against all odds.

People would tell me that I am a great mom; so patient and understanding, and that I am unique to be "sacrificing" my time. My response is that I am doing what a mom is supposed to do out of love and care for her child.

Aren't moms supposed to fight tooth and nail to make sure their kids live their best lives?

Aren't moms supposed to give their all and search the world for what their children need?

I don't think what I did was anything special; I did what I had to do to keep this child on track and happy and made sure I left no stone unturned for the help we needed. It was my privilege and pleasure, although tough, but a pleasure to be doing this for my son. A lively, fun, risky, loud child with so much spirit– so full of life and emotion.

I initially adopted my mom's parenting style, which was 'when I say sit, you sit'—a style I wouldn't recommend now, as I believe children should be treated with more respect. And the older two sat! This one did not sit!

My third child is the one who changed my life, the one who wouldn't accept 'no' without a full explanation. I quickly learned the phrase "positive reinforcement." This made me realise that the world is full of judgmental people, and I was probably one of them! I learned that people have differences that must be respected, and the greatest lesson I learned was that one must always be kind to others, no matter how they may be acting, as we don't know what their lives are like or what they may be going through. This was, at that time and many times afterward, a reflection of myself.

I could be talking to someone, and the only thing going through my mind was, "How am I going to get my son to school tomorrow? Will he ever graduate high school? Will he ever go to college? Will he get a job? Will he be invited to the next birthday party?"

ADHD and extreme generalised anxiety didn't have a place in Hong Kong schools other than being labelled as naughty, lazy, or being told he doesn't have a choice. When my anxious 10-year-old refused to enter school, kicking and screaming, I finally gave in. It became my life's mission to educate myself on anxiety, ADHD, and oppositional defiance through books, psychologists, psychiatrists, parent groups, counsellors, parent advocates, and parenting classes. I built my own Individual Education Plans and accommodations; I didn't let anyone or anything stand in my way. My child was going to have the best education with teachers who respected him, and I would be there to make sure of that. Standing guard, dismissing judgments, and building my spine of steel, I was a mom on a mission to advocate for my son.

This crusade of mine, consisting of me and me alone, was full of mixed emotions: loneliness, hopelessness, sometimes feeling deflated, but also empowered, determined, and invincible!

I withdrew from many social situations because I didn't want to meet people who didn't understand what I was going through. Someone could be talking about the state of the world, and I would be thinking about my next step in getting my son to open his mouth at the dentist. It was all-consuming, but I didn't see this as a sacrifice, which is what many would label it as. I viewed it as my privilege as a mom. It was hard, but I gained strength and determination through all the love and protection a mother feels for her children.

Through this journey, I found the "angels" who supported us—the dentist who allowed my son to come in twice just to look around, ask questions, and touch all the instruments. He let my son bring his own movie to watch during the procedures and explained everything step by step, answering all questions without hesitation and pausing when prompted. There were also the teachers who understood our struggles and supported us through home-schooling, allowing us to come in whenever my son was ready. The tutoring centre tailored a full school day for him, and the psychologist never gave up, guiding me every step of the way. Of course the friends standing on the wayside waiting for a chance to jump in and help.

It's crucial to find these "angels" to help in such situations, most importantly, the ones living at home in the thick of it. My two older kids were incredibly supportive, helpful, and patient throughout this journey. My husband, the loving dad, was thrown into this whirlwind with us. He supported us as best he could, acting as co-captain, which suited us well. He was always there when needed, sometimes just to catch us when we fell.

Sometimes, when you're searching for answers, you come across an outlier. I heard someone speak at a TEDx presentation on education and was completely inspired by his speech about learning differently. He was the principal of a school in the UK, and I asked him for a coffee. His first question, after hearing my story and my despair with school, was life-changing. It stopped me in my tracks and was something I had never considered before.

"Why is it so important to you that your son attends a traditional school every day?"

This was a loaded question that got me thinking: Why

does he have to attend school? By this time, he was 15 years old, just starting his GCSEs, and experiencing so much anxiety that he could not make it to school. He studied hard at home, tried to keep up with all his classes, and received all the work from his teachers to do on his own. He was up to date on school, world events, and, being the engineer that he is, he knew everything about everything—from why a bird flies up or down to how to build a 3D printer.

Why is "school," the traditional institution created over 400 years ago, still considered the correct pathway for all kids? This question prompted me to think deeply, and I decided to take a leap of faith.

That leap of faith was the right decision, just as all the others before and after it were. I did fall flat on my face with a few attempts and probably set us back a few steps, but I chose to leap forward and consider it a learning process.

My intuition and gut feeling, along with my love and respect for my child, were all I needed. Together, we cleared the path ahead.

A key point is that "I took the back seat while he got into the driver's seat, and he has been driving ever since into the next decade. There have been some bumps along the way, but those bumps build character and prepare you for life's experiences." Sometimes when we are too engrossed in our kids' lives and keep trying to "fix" things, we can actually cause damage. We need to find that balance.

The values my older kids witnessed throughout this journey are immeasurable. They see our struggles, learn from our resilience, and feel the strength of our bond. I see this not only in their personal lives but also in their professional values. My daughter has since gone on to become a clinical psychologist working in Hong Kong, helping children and adults see the colour and strength of diversity.

It's the "spirited" kids—the ones who can't hear "no," who push boundaries, the risk-takers and the autonomous ones—who, if guided gently and respectfully, will change the world.

As I reflect on our journey with my son, it becomes clear that the traditional educational system often overlooks the unique needs of children like him—those with ADHD, anxiety, and other learning differences. For many, school is not just a place of learning but a battleground where they struggle with social and academic challenges. The conventional classroom approach often clashes with various learning styles, creating frustration and low self-esteem. This journey, and others like it, can demonstrate the greatness and resilience of these kids when given the right settings and accommodations to thrive.

Executive function skills, which are primarily governed by the prefrontal cortex, play a major role in a child's ability to navigate school. These skills—organisation, processing speed, working memory, emotional regulation, planning, focus, and time management—are crucial for success in school and daily life. The prefrontal cortex of the brain does not fully develop until about 26 years old, and kids with ADHD are generally three to five years behind. This developmental delay is a major factor that can cause high anxiety in these children and potentially lead to school refusal.

For parents of children with ADHD, understanding the importance of educational, and psychological assessments is crucial for effective learning and emotional well-being. These assessments provide a comprehensive evaluation of a child's cognitive abilities, strengths, and challenges, particularly concerning executive function skills. By obtaining this assessment, parents can gain valuable insights into their child's specific needs, allowing for tailored interventions that make both school and home life more manageable.

Accommodations based on these assessments can significantly enhance a child's learning experience. For instance:

- Organisational challenges can be addressed through the use of visual schedules and color-coded folders that help children keep track of assignments and materials.

- Strategies to improve processing speed may include extended time for tests and assignments, allowing children to demonstrate their knowledge without the pressure of strict time limits.

- Working memory issues can be mitigated by using mnemonic devices or by breaking down tasks into smaller, more manageable steps.

- Furthermore, emotional regulation can be supported by implementing calming techniques, such as mindfulness exercises or designated quiet spaces in the classroom and at home, where children can regroup when feeling overwhelmed.

This experience led me to my new career path over a decade ago. I am a certified parent coach and teacher trainer working with parents, teachers, and counsellors on positive communication with children. I utilise universal, scientifically backed communication skills such as active listening, collaborative problem-solving, and preventive "I" messages, to name a few, which are effective with all kids. This approach is particularly beneficial for children with ADHD and mild learning differences, as these children are often sensitive and spirited. They thrive on respect and clear communication, which helps them feel understood and valued.

In conclusion, this journey has not only transformed my life but also equipped me with the tools to support others in their parenting and teaching efforts. By fostering positive communication, we can create environments where children feel safe expressing themselves and exploring their potential. I hope that through this work, we can empower both children and adults to navigate their challenges together, building stronger relationships and fostering resilience and success in the process.

ABOUT THE AUTHOR

Shalini Melwani is a compassionate and experienced parent consultant and coach with a deep personal and professional commitment to helping families. A proud mom of three adult children, she brings both lived experience and specialised expertise to her practice. She teaches parents how to foster better communication, resolve conflicts, and build healthier relationships with their children. Her approach empowers parents to be both compassionate and effective in their parenting roles.

Shalini is a certified ADHD Parent Coach and a dedicated Parent Advocate. She works extensively with parents raising children with Attention Deficit Hyperactivity Disorder (ADHD) and other mild learning differences. With her guidance, parents gain the tools to advocate for their children's educational and emotional needs, ensuring they receive the appropriate support both at school and in other settings. Through her multifaceted work, Shalini has become a trusted resource for parents and has left a lasting impact on the communities she serves.

YOU CAN CONNECT WITH SHALINI AT:

LinkedIn: *https://www.linkedin.com/in/shalinimelwani/*
Website: *www.parentingempowered.com*
Email: *shalini@parentingempowered.com*

Story Seventeen

THE REBIRTH

A Journey of Resilience and Renewal.

It was 2021, and we were slowly emerging from the shadows of COVID-19, cautiously reclaiming fragments of normalcy.

For me, this time marked the culmination of a seven-year journey: I had defended my doctorate, fulfilling a dream I had pursued with unwavering perseverance.

Being a part-time graduate student while juggling family, work, and personal growth is a solitary endeavour. My evenings, weekends, and vacations had been consumed by research and study, leaving little room for anything else. The lack of immediate support from my university added to the weight I carried. This wasn't unique to me but rather was shared by many other courageous students who juggle family responsibilities and full-time work as they chase their academic aspirations.

When my thesis was finally approved, I expected a wave of fulfilment. Instead of the triumph I anticipated, I felt an unexpected void. And with the absence of a celebratory moment, a stage to cross, or a handshake with peers left me with a hollow sense of incompleteness. The celebration that would have marked the completion of this chapter was stolen by the pandemic.

This lack of closure weighed heavily on me. I soon realised I wasn't alone in these feelings; many people face an inexplicable void after reaching a hard-earned peak. The real challenge lies in navigating what comes next. I had always been resilient, a climber of literal and metaphorical mountains, and I knew the descent was often harder than the climb. But this wasn't just a mountain - it was my life.

Something was lost. I needed clarity, and I needed space to find it.

Sometimes, finding clarity requires stepping away. In October of that year, I decided to embark on a journey, an escape to Konya, Turkey, the city of Rumi. Konya is deeply tied to the legacy of Jalal al-Din Rumi, the 13th-century Persian poet and Sufi mystic. His teachings on love, spirituality, and the search for deeper meaning were exactly what my soul needed. Rumi's timeless wisdom speaks to looking inward for answers. One of his most powerful teachings, "What you seek is seeking you," called out to me. For someone feeling lost and adrift, his words served as a beacon, urging me to quiet the noise of the outside world and tune in to my own inner voice. I hoped that perhaps, in Konya, I could find what I was truly seeking.

In the heart of Konya, I allowed myself to sit with the silence, to walk the cobbled streets, to watch the dervishes whirl in their endless dance of devotion, each movement symbolising the shedding of ego and surrender. It was in these moments of stillness, surrounded by Rumi's teachings, that I began to unravel my emotions and allow myself to feel deeply once more.

My guide during my days in Konya was a gift, as you will understand later in my story. She was knowledgeable about everything Rumi. She also possessed the peace I was seeking in my own soul. Such sensations are contagious - when you are surrounded by peace, you feel at peace.

My days in Konya provided the silence and peace I needed, but the answers remained elusive. I needed more than stillness; I needed movement and freedom. And so, I left Konya for Cappadocia, the land of wild horses, as the name itself means.

Cappadocia felt like stepping into another world - a landscape both ancient and otherworldly, a testament to nature's artistry. The fairy chimneys, tall and surreal, rose from the earth like guardians of the past. The coloured valleys and the painted sky, with hot air balloons floating against the backdrop of the rising sun, created a burst of colour and life.

Adventure lurked around every corner, from hiking through valleys with whimsical names like Love Valley and Rose Valley to horseback riding across the plains at sunset. Cappadocia is a place of mystical beauty, where one cannot help but feel humbled by the landscape. My hotel room, a cave transformed into a luxurious haven, was an enchanting blend of history and comfort, like something out of a fairytale. As I stood on the terrace, watching hot air balloons rise with the sun, I felt a surge of hope, a reminder that life, in all its unpredictability, always holds magic. Between the mystical Konya and the majestic Cappadocia, I started to find myself again.

I had planned my days there carefully: hot air ballooning before sunrise, horseback riding at sunset, and three full days of hiking across the valleys. I was eager to experience the hot air balloon ride the next day before sunrise. In Konya, I learned how to sit still in harmony with myself. Here, I wanted to be in harmony with the majestic place I was in.

I wanted to experience the world from new heights, to feel connected to the earth beneath me. As the sun rose over Cappadocia, I floated among the hot air balloons, the world below bathed in golden light. It was breathtaking, an experience that spoke of freedom, of perspective, of the beauty in simply being. And it was in this moment, high above the earth, that I found my first answer: my life was filled with blessings that I had overlooked. I had so much to give, and I knew then that my purpose was to share these gifts. It was a moment of total bliss.

But fate had more lessons in store for me. In the afternoon, I mounted a horse, ready for a leisurely ride at sunset. I had always loved horses - their strength and elegance - and I felt at ease. We began the ride, crossing the valleys and climbing the cliffs, basking in the beauty of the fading sun. Everything felt perfect until it wasn't.

Without warning, my horse, spooked by something unseen, bolted. He ran fast, faster than I could control. I pulled the reins and tried to calm him, but fear had taken over. In a flash, and before I knew it, I was thrown from the horse, hitting the ground hard and rolling until I landed painfully on my side. The world spun, my body ached, and I found myself lying there, unable to move, staring at the sky above.

The guide rushed to help, but the pain was unbearable. My helmet had fallen off, and my leg wouldn't move. We waited for hours for an ambulance, stranded in the valley beneath the darkening sky. While lying on the ground, I suddenly noticed I had lost one shoe. It's amazing how the brain works when traumatised - of all things, I became fixated on finding my shoe. I even demanded that the guide search for it. I later discovered that the shoe was stuck with the horse; imagine if my leg had been stuck along with it!

In those hours, as the cold set in, I found myself surrendering completely—not to fear, but to the moment. "Oh God," I whispered over and over in total calmness. I was aware of what had happened and accepted it deeply. The paramedics arrived, and I was taken to a local hospital, where I learned the extent of my injuries: my sacrum was broken, and my back cracked. I was far from home, alone, and unable to walk.

That night in the local hospital was the longest I had ever experienced. The staff barely spoke English and provided minimal care and medication. Unable to move on my own, I waited for the next day's thorough medical examination and finalisation of arrangements to fly me back to Dubai while lying on my back. I needed someone to be with me, and the only person I could think to call was my guide from Konya. She arrived with her husband and stayed by my side, comforting me with her presence. Before I left Turkey, she told me something that became engraved in my heart: "Let this be your rebirth. Never go back to life as usual."

With those words, I returned home in an air ambulance, with a body that could not walk and a heart that had started to heal. I spent two months on my back, in pain, unable to do the simplest things. Yet, those months became some of the most blessed times of my life. I found joy in the smallest victories: in the first steps, I managed to take, in the sunsets I watched from my window, in the friends who visited constantly, in the family who loved me, in the first walk I was able to take by the beach. I learned to surrender to what was, to accept life not as a series of achievements but as a collection of moments - moments of pain, of joy, of connection. I was grateful every day.

Halfway through my recovery, the university informed us about a small winter graduation ceremony. I was still bedridden, but I asked my doctor if there was a chance I could attend. I expected a negative response, but instead received a "Why not?" I might need crutches or a wheelchair, but I could make it. And so, I said yes, not knowing what the next month would bring. But I wanted it - I wanted that closure, that moment to acknowledge all that had led me here.

In December 2021, just two months after my fall, I travelled to the University in the UK for my graduation. Draped in my graduation robe, the fluffy graduation hat on my head, and despite my cracked back and broken sacrum, I walked across the stage to accept my degree from the chancellor. In that moment, I felt the void inside me shift, not because I had found closure, but because I had found a new beginning. My guide's words echoed in my mind: "Make this moment your rebirth." As I glanced into the audience and saw my daughter's tear-filled eyes brimming with pride, I understood that I was neither broken nor lost. I had been reborn.

As I reflect on the emptiness I felt after earning my doctorate, I now see that void not as a loss but as a space waiting to be filled with growth, gratitude, and a deeper understanding of life's purpose. What I sought in Konya and found through my struggles was not just healing but transformation.

This journey, with all its pain and beauty, taught me profound lessons about life and resilience. I learned that life is not about one peak or one achievement; life is a journey of peaks and valleys, of moments that test us and moments that lift us higher than we could imagine. I learned that earning my degree was not the culmination but rather a doorway to new beginnings. I learned that the pain of falling, though profound, is a reminder of our resilience and our ability to rise stronger. I learned to find gratitude in the smallest moments. I learned that my strength wasn't in pushing myself to achieve more; it was in accepting my vulnerability and embracing every part of my story, even the broken pieces.

To those like me who felt at one point in their lives lost or unfulfilled after reaching a milestone, remember: the void isn't an ending; it's an opening. The emptiness you feel after an achievement is not a loss but a space inviting you to redefine your purpose and explore new horizons. Reflect on what this space is inviting you to fill. What blessings have you overlooked? What doors can you now open? Take a moment to listen to your inner voice, seek stillness or move away if needed, and most importantly, trust in the beauty of life's peaks and valleys. Every triumph, every challenge, and every fall is a chance to write the next chapter of your story. This is your journey; let it unfold.

ABOUT THE AUTHOR

Dr. **Dina Faidi** is the founder of Creativity & Beyond Consulting Firm (UAE) and a highly accomplished global leader in executive education, innovation, design thinking, leadership, cognitive behaviour, and human skills development. With over 28 years of professional experience and a doctorate in education, Dr. Dina seamlessly integrates academic expertise with practical knowledge to deliver tailored solutions through consulting, teaching, facilitation, coaching, and mentoring. She collaborates with leaders, entrepreneurs, and government officials, while championing women's empowerment and driving societal change through innovation and mentorship.

Dr. Dina is also deeply committed to social responsibility, actively educating, mentoring, and inspiring youth and women through partnerships with social enterprises and NGOs. Her passion for societal impact is evident in her role as an advisory board member of **Challenge to Change (CTC)**. In 2024, Dina co-authored the Amazon No.1

Bestselling book, #MyVoice Vol.8 and won the prestigious Global Women of Influence Award for her contribution to society.

YOU CAN CONNECT WITH DR. DINA AT:

LinkedIn: *https://www.linkedin.com/in/dinafaidi-edd/*
Email: *dina.faidi@gmail.com*

Story Eighteen

UNSPOKEN

Whispers of the Wombs.

As I lay in the delivery room, gripping my mother's hand amidst unbearable labour pain, anger swelled within me. She never prepared me for this—never warned me of the excruciating ordeal. I saw the unspoken guilt in her eyes, her helplessness rooted in her own struggles. "If I had told you how painful it is, you would have been frightened," she whispered softly in those vulnerable moments.

THE NEWBORNS - MOTHER-DAUGHTER: WELCOMED BY ANOTHER

Cut to the homecoming moment for the two newborns—my daughter and the mother within me—both brought to life in that transformative moment.

Arriving at my mother's doorstep, we shared an ethereal, goddess-like moment. Lakshmi and Saraswati welcomed us home, showering us with their love and blessings.

Lakshmi and Saraswati were not merely goddesses of wealth and virtue that I had read about in mythology. I metaphorically referred to my grandmother Shanti as Lakshmi, who symbolised the strength and abundance she brought to the family, and my mother Revati as Saraswati, who instilled values, wisdom, and holistic education in our family.

As for me, becoming a mother brought me to a pivotal crossroads—a tug-of-war between career aspirations and the desire to be present for my child. My motherhood journey had collided with a turbulent work situation.

This chapter explores the challenging choices women face between professional ambitions and personal responsibilities, examined through the lens of motherhood. It reflects on how a prolonged career break transformed my perspective on life's choices from black and white to a more nuanced understanding.

WHERE IT ALL BEGAN: A JOURNEY ACROSS BORDERS, INTO THE UNKNOWN

When I moved to Singapore after marriage, it felt like a fresh start—a blank canvas on which to paint my dreams. But as the months passed, reality began to set in. Despite countless job applications and relentless efforts, my career seemed stuck. Work permits, visa issues, and unanswered applications drained my confidence, leaving me questioning my abilities. Regret crept into the cracks of my new life, and I began to wonder whether moving overseas had cost me my career.

Just as I began to lose hope, I received an offer from a top-tier multinational company. The joy of securing the job was short-lived, however, as I discovered I was pregnant just two days later. The timing felt like a cruel twist of fate—two life-changing events arrived simultaneously, leaving me torn between them.

I followed the flow.

DAY ONE: TURBULENCE - THE RIDE BEGINS

On my first day at work, excitement turned to dread. My supervisor discovered that HR had elevated my job title during the hiring process based on my years of experience, placing me at her level. Her resentment was palpable, and it quickly spiralled into hostility. I felt the tension mounting but hesitated to reveal my pregnancy. Each day became a battlefield, with her ego overshadowing the work.

Barely a month into the job, facing long hours and a difficult boss, I had to draw on what had defined me all my life—courage!

CAREER OR CRADLE? AN INTERSECTION OF AMBITION AND SELFLESSNESS

"Should I postpone motherhood? Would my organisation regret hiring me?" Such thoughts consumed me as career ambitions took precedence. Motherhood felt like a battle to fight.

The joy in my family over the baby news overshadowed everything else. With my spouse's unwavering support, I gained more clarity about embracing motherhood as a priority. When I informed my supervisor about my pregnancy, her response was sharp: "But this doesn't look like maternity attire." What followed was a campaign of isolation and intimidation that turned the workplace into a hostile environment.

A colleague confided that she could no longer interact with me openly, revealing that no one had survived under this supervisor's leadership in the past seven years. During a fire drill, I stood briefly with my husband, who worked in the same organisation. When I returned to my desk, my supervisor interrogated me. "Do I need approval for who I stand with now?" I snapped, annoyed.

Her need for control intensified, and days later, she handed me a list of tasks with a bizarre restriction: I could only obtain information from her. Frustrated, I appealed to senior leaders, questioning how I could perform effectively under such constraints. Their response? Silence. The supervisor's seven years of tenure held more weight than my two months at the company. As a pregnant newcomer, I became an easy target. The realisation hit hard—organisations sometimes prioritise egos over people.

TURMOIL WITHIN: THE FIRST TRIMESTER TRIALS

Three months into my pregnancy, I reached a breaking point. I had to make a choice: fight for my career or embrace the life growing within me. My husband urged me to walk away from the toxicity.

It felt like surrendering to injustice. Unaware of the lasting impact of womb trauma, I didn't realise my child was already absorbing that emotional landscape.

The first trimester was like fighting a battle on two fronts, and I could no longer delay taking corrective and decisive action to break free from this cycle.

UNDER FIRE: PERSISTENCE AND COURAGE WON THE BATTLE FOR THE RIGHT

On my last day, I stood my ground, confronting the situation head-on with unwavering courage. I meticulously detailed each incident to management, urging them to prioritise employee well-being and implement necessary changes. A senior leader, moved by my resolve, recognised the courage of a pregnant woman standing firm amidst the chaos. This moment marked the beginning of my journey toward true empathy—an understanding that only motherhood could teach me.

As I walked away from that toxic environment, I felt liberated. By standing firm, I had learned a valuable lesson in self-respect and courage.

After I left my job, the prospect of new motherhood became a comforting promise—a solace I clung to in search of happiness.

Uncannily, this struggle mirrored the conflicting traits of my mother and grandmother, which I had unknowingly internalised. Vastly different yet bound by blood, they created a sense of timelessness during that phase, when I most strongly understood the depth of this connection, realising how the emotional imprint of their lives had profoundly shaped my own.

Their influence subtly guided me throughout my nine-month pregnancy and beyond.

These reflections form the core of this chapter, explored in depth in the pages ahead.

I pause now to revisit their story, which was lost for decades and resonated with me as I began navigating motherhood.

Stay with me!

THE PAGES LEFT BEHIND: A LEGACY WRITTEN IN TIME...

In her final days, my grandmother scribbled parts of her life story, which my mother later pieced together. She had named her autobiography "*Dhoop Chaon*" (Sunshine & Shadow), capturing her journey from a child bride to a widowed young woman, and ultimately, a village leader and educator.

Reading my grandmother's autobiography still tears me apart!

At just 13, she had gotten married. Her husband was a visionary scholar-engineer working on special British-assigned projects, including the Sharda Dam, the last major British colonial irrigation project in India. He dreamed of transforming their village in Ranikhet through education and was determined to complete her education—a promise that became urgent as his health failed and more desperate when he realised his life was ending soon. Tragically, he passed away when she was just 17, leaving her a young widow with a 3-year-old daughter.

Against all odds, she fulfilled his wish. She pursued higher education, became a teacher, rose through the ranks to become a school head, and even served as a village chief. Such a feat was extraordinary for a woman in that era.

On the other hand, her daughter's role in completing and complementing her mother's story was more than a duty—it was an extension of the whispers she had heard in her mother's womb, guiding her even after her mother's passing.

Connecting the dots, my mother's life was equally shaped by extraordinary circumstances. At just 3 years old, she lost her father and became a pillar for her teenage mother. With only a 15-year age gap, she sacrificed her childhood to nurture and support her mother, whose focus was on expanding her education and building a career as the sole breadwinner.

In essence, the daughter became the nurturer, a mother to her own mother.

PROMISE OF THREE

On my grandmother's first death anniversary, my mother distributed her autobiography in her homeland, revealing herself not just as a nurturer but as the custodian of a legacy she helped complete. Through her, the silent whispers of strength and sacrifice were passed on to me.

Reflecting now, I see myself as a voice for their whispers, reviving their stories—first through publishing my grandmother's autobiography and now through this chapter. My own journey, from stepping back for motherhood to reclaiming a career after two decades, was shaped by my grandmother's courage and my mother's selfless nurturing. Their influence continues to guide me

MY WOMB LESSONS

- **Strength is Multifaceted**
  Ambition and selflessness can coexist in their own unique ways.

  My grandmother's fiery ambition and independence stood in stark contrast to my mother's selflessness. Both women embodied virtues that defined their unique strengths - contrasting yet powerful qualities.

- **Life reveals its purposes in unexpected ways.**
  Whether through regret or awakening, the stories of our lineage shape us.

  Bringing my grandmother's autobiography to life, I watched my mother's dormant writing talent bloom in her seventies, proving that life reveals its purpose when we're ready.

  My challenging first overseas experience became a lesson in courage and resilience, shaping me at life's crossroads. That turbulent start evolved into certification in strength, empowering me to rise, reclaim what was mine, and build a thriving career spanning over 20 years—a testament to life's power to transform hardship into growth.

- **XX Factor**
  Motherhood gave me a fresh perspective on a pivotal choice. I wrestled with the unspoken but profound contrasting influences that my mother and grandmother had on me.

  The extended time after childbirth provided clarity through introspection. What had once seemed like a conflict between my grandmother's career resilience and my mother's selflessness revealed itself as complementary strengths. My black-and-white lens shifted, uncovering a spectrum of vibrant truths to embrace.

This deepened my belief that every woman possesses an extraordinary X factor, derived from the unparalleled strength of her XX chromosomes, both biologically and mentally.

EPILOGUE: WHISPERS OF THE WOMBS

The lessons of the womb are quiet whispers that shape our lives across generations.

We must listen to these unspoken whispers intuitively and uncover their purpose. Whether from those who silently hold up the sky for others or those in the spotlight, both have stories that deserve to be seen and heard—passed from womb to womb.

My grandmother's immensely successful professional life lacked the deep relationship bonds that she saw fulfilled in her daughter's life. In contrast, my mother rarely experienced the outside world. Her life revolved around serving her mother, husband, and children. Together, they completed each other's journeys, giving and receiving what the other lacked.

Looking back at their lives, I reflect on my own choices through the lens of responsibility, striving to fulfil the promise of three generations as it was meant to be.

Through this chapter, I have aspired to share the wisdom of unspoken whispers passed down through wombs, honouring the promise and legacy of past generations. It is my humble contribution, a small drop in the vast ocean of shaken, stirred, but undeterred stories meant to inspire, uplift and endure.

ABOUT THE AUTHOR

Based in Singapore, **Sonia J Arora** balances her dual passions as a film scriptwriter alongside a successful corporate career with global exposure. She seamlessly blends creativity with commerce, redefining philanthropy by aligning it with purpose.

Her screenplay, Misfits, has achieved global recognition, winning Best Script Award at the London Film Festival, an Honourable Mention at the Tokyo Screenplay Awards, and an Official Selection at the Hollywood Stage Script Competition. Her debut film as a writer, Love, Yours Truly, won over 12 international awards. Sonia co-authored #MyVoice Vol. 4 for the Singapore Children's Society and was runner-up in Singapore's Zee Talent Hunt.

An advocate for creativity, compassion, and women's and children's rights, Sonia received the Global Women of Influence Award 2024 and another Global Award in her organisation for work with a Singapore NGO. As Co-

Founding Director of a Delhi-based NGO, she aspires to craft meaningful stories, spreading hope and joy globally.

YOU CAN CONNECT WITH SONIA AT:

LinkedIn: *https://www.linkedin.com/in/soniajarora/*
Email: *soniajoshi.arora@gmail.com*

RAISING YOUR VOICE

We all have an opinion, a view or simply, thoughts about things that happen to or around us. Some think, some speak, but the majority do nothing.

But what if you are the one who does something about it and takes charge of a situation, turning challenges into inspiration? Don't you want to be heard and even help those who don't dare to speak? Wouldn't you want to be remembered forever?

Writing a book is a guaranteed way to build a strong personal brand, boost your market value, and be seen as an authority in your domain. But what it also does is helps you leave a legacy that will last forever whether you become famous or not!

GLOBAL INFLUENCERS PUBLISHING HOUSE, is a Singapore-based independent publisher that specialises in non-fiction and literary works that can be inspirational, knowledge-based, or simply enjoyable to read.

Our objective is to connect the hearts and minds of international readers and authors through the power of words. With the support of a highly skilled and dedicated team, carefully chosen for their exceptional talent and passion to achieve new heights, they work tirelessly behind the scenes to create something extraordinary.

Our mission is to empower authors to share their unique stories, insights, thoughts, feelings, emotions, and expertise with the world. Whether it's a memoir, a self-help guide, a business book, or a novel, we strive to publish works that are impactful and thought-provoking.

Our belief is that everyone creates and retells their own narrative. And through it, if you are able to make a lasting impression for future generations, that is what matters. So, if you too have a **STORY** to share and you want create your legacy by writing about it, send us a message on:
shikha@globalinfluencers.sg

You can also join the **#MY VOICE FORUM**, which provides a network for like-minded women worldwide to come together to talk about things that matter. A safe space where we can agree, disagree, or agree to disagree but without any judgement, discuss issues and challenges faced, lend a listening ear or a helping hand to one another, find solutions and ultimately take action to make change happen.

To find out more, go to: **www.facebook.com/groups/myvoiceforum**

"Together we will embark on a new journey by creating the world we deserve to live in." - *Neera Gupta, Chief Visionary Officer at Global Influencers Publishing House.*

GLOBAL WOMEN OF INFLUENCE AWARDS 2025

COMING SOON

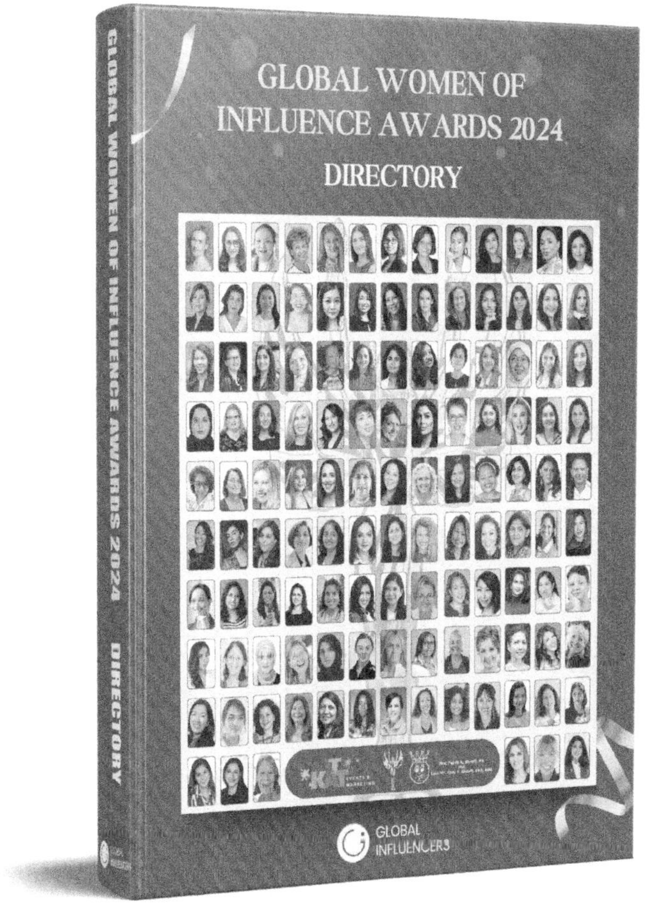

Made in the USA
Middletown, DE
13 March 2025

72644067R00134